IF YOU BITE & DEVOUR ONE ANOTHER

Galatians 5:15

Other books by Alexander Strauch include:

Biblical Eldership:
An Urgent Call to Restore Biblical Church Leadership

The Study Guide to Biblical Eldership:
Twelve Lessons for Mentoring Men for Eldership

Meetings That Work

Paul's Vision for the Deacons:
Assisting the Elders with the Care of God's Church

The Hospitality Commands

Agape Leadership:
Lessons in Spiritual Leadership from the Life of
R.C. Chapman (Coauthored with Robert L. Peterson)

Men and Women: Equal Yet Different

A Christian Leader's Guide to Leading with Love

Love or Die:
Christ's Wake-Up Call to the Church, Revelation 2:4

The 15 Descriptions of Love:
Applied to All Christian Leaders & Teachers

√ F. SCHAEFFER PG 24

IF YOU BITE & DEVOUR ONE ANOTHER

Galatians 5:15

Biblical Principles for Handling Conflict

Alexander Strauch

Lewis & Roth Publishers

If You Bite & Devour One Another
ISBN-10: 093608331X
ISBN-13: 9780936083315
Copyright © 2011 by Alexander Strauch. All rights reserved.

Cover design: Eric Anderson (www.resolutiondesign.com)

Printed in the United States of America
Sixth Printing 2019

Library of Congress Control Number: 2010943137

To receive a free catalog of books published by Lewis and Roth Publishers, please call toll free 800-477-3239 or visit our website, *www.lewisandroth.org*. If you are calling from outside the United States, please call 719-494-1800.

Lewis and Roth Publishers
P.O. Box 469
Littleton, Colorado 80160

Contents

Abbreviations

1. Old Testament

Gen.	Genesis	Ezra	Ezra	Dan.	Daniel
Ex.	Exodus	Neh.	Nehemiah	Hos.	Hosea
Lev.	Leviticus	Est.	Esther	Joel	Joel
Num.	Numbers	Job	Job	Amos	Amos
Deut.	Deuteronomy	Ps.	Psalm(s)	Obad.	Obadiah
Josh.	Joshua	Prov.	Proverbs	Jonah	Jonah
Judg.	Judges	Eccl.	Ecclesiastes	Mic.	Micah
Ruth	Ruth	Song.	Song of Solomon	Nah.	Nahum
1 Sam.	1 Samuel	Isa.	Isaiah	Hab.	Habakkuk
2 Sam.	2 Samuel	Jer.	Jeremiah	Zeph.	Zephaniah
1 Kings	1 Kings	Lam.	Lamentations	Hag.	Haggai
2 Kings	2 Kings	Ezek.	Ezekiel	Zech.	Zechariah
1 Chron.	1 Chronicles			Mal.	Malachi
2 Chron.	2 Chronicles				

2. New Testament

Matt.	Matthew	Phil.	Philippians	James	James
Mark	Mark	Col.	Colossians	1 Peter	1 Peter
Luke	Luke	1 Thess.	1 Thessalonians	2 Peter	2 Peter
John	John	2 Thess.	2 Thessalonians	1 John	1 John
Acts	Acts of the Apostles	1 Tim.	1 Timothy	2 John	2 John
Rom.	Romans	2 Tim.	2 Timothy	3 John	3 John
1 Cor.	1 Corinthians	Titus	Titus	Jude	Jude
2 Cor.	2 Corinthians	Philem.	Philemon	Rev.	The Revelation
Gal.	Galatians	Heb.	Hebrews		to John
Eph.	Ephesians				(Apocalypse)

3. Books	
BDAG	W. Bauer, W.F. Arndt, F.W. Gingrich, and F.W. Danker, *Greek-English Lexicon of the New Testament* (3rd ed.)
BECNT	Baker Exegetical Commentary on the New Testament
BST	The Bible Speaks Today
ESV	English Standard Version
IVP	InterVarsity Press
NAC	New American Commentary
NCB	New Century Bible
NIBC	New International Bible Commentary on the New Testament
NICNT	New International Commentary on the New Testament
NICOT	New International Commentary on the Old Testament
NIGTC	New International Greek Testament Commentary
NIV	New International Version
NPNF	Nicene and Post-Nicene Fathers
NTC	New Testament Commentary
PNTC	The Pillar New Testament Commentary
TDNT	G. Kittel and G. Friedrich (eds.), *Theological Dictionary of the New Testament*
TNTC	Tyndale New Testament Commentary
TOTC	Tyndale Old Testament Commentary
UBS	United Bible Society (4th ed.)
WBC	Word Biblical Commentary
WEC	Wycliffe Exegetical Commentary
ZECNT	Zondervan Exegetical Commentary on the New Testament

Introduction

Be completely humble and gentle; be patient, bearing with one another in
love. Make every effort to keep the unity of the Spirit through the
bond of peace.
Ephesians 4:2-3 (NIV)

The moment Adam and Eve sinned, the peace and unity of paradise was lost. Their sin immediately threw them into conflict—Adam blaming Eve and Eve blaming the serpent for their sinful actions. Their sin initiated the war of the sexes. Disunity rather than unity came to characterize the human race. Life in the world became life in a battlefield. ·· THIS DEVICE OF SATANS

Human conflict is one of the dreadful consequences of sin entering the world. Because of sin, all human relationships are a struggle and are prone to conflict. We can trace the unrelenting plague of human conflict through the endless wars and divisions of human history, and sadly, church history as well. Throughout Scripture we see the ugly reality of sin displayed in cruel wars and fighting even among those who are called to be God's people:

—The first sin recorded after Adam and Eve were driven from the garden is that of Cain killing his brother Abel. Jealousy, out-of-control anger, selfish ambition, and pride drove Cain to hate and kill his brother (Gen. 4:8).

—While still in the womb, the twin brothers Jacob and Esau struggled for dominance (Gen. 25:22).

—Jealousy over their younger brother's favorite-son status with their father drove ten of Jacob's twelve sons to sell Joseph into slavery and to deceive their father into thinking that he was dead (Gen. 37:18-33).

—For years in the wilderness desert, the children of Israel relentlessly criticized and stubbornly resisted Moses' leadership. At one point Moses wanted to die because of their non-stop complaining (Num. 11:14-15).

—Saul, Israel's first king, was a proud man. His insane jealousy over the success of David, a young military leader, led him to commit nearly every social sin condemned in God's law. Instead of rejoicing that he had such a competent junior leader, Saul did all in his power to kill the competition (1 Sam. 15:12; 18:6-16).

—Late in King David's reign, his son Absalom charmed the nation into abandoning their king. Absalom intended to kill his own godly father and usurp his God-given throne. Absalom's lust for power and selfish ambition drove him to deceit and murder (2 Sam. 15).

—King Solomon's sin of idolatry shattered Israel's unity and divided the nation into two warring kingdoms—each with its own king, place of worship, and priesthood (1 Kings 12).

—The New Testament gives witness to the awful struggle between Israel's religious leaders and Jesus the Messiah. Out of hate and jealousy over Christ's exposure of their hypocritical, self-righteous behavior, Israel's leaders "killed the Author of life" (Acts 3:15).

—During his earthly life, our Lord had to deal with selfish ambition among his disciples when they quarreled over who among them was the greatest and who would be enthroned at his side (Mark 9:34; 10:37). How would they ever work together in unity after their Master's death?

Fast forward to today. How are Christians to work together in unity until Jesus comes again? The answer to this question is foundational to our understanding of how to deal with conflict according to biblical principles. Jesus taught the unique principles of humility, servanthood, forgiveness, and love, and he promised to send a helper to enable his disciples to live by his teaching. So at Pentecost, following Jesus' death, resurrection, and ascension, God sent the Holy Spirit down from heaven to indwell all believers. By the enabling power of the Holy Spirit and obedience to Jesus' teachings, his disciples were able to work together in harmony as the first Christian leadership body. However, the coming of the Holy Spirit didn't eliminate all fighting or controversy among the Spirit-indwelt people of God. The churches of the New Testament period still experienced plenty of conflict. *As the inspired New Testament writers addressed these matters, they provided invaluable instruction on how Christian believers are to think, act, and treat one another when conflict arises.* By studying the Scripture, we can learn how God would have us live in harmony even when we disagree with one another.

It is helpful to keep in mind that there is nothing wrong with Christians disagreeing with one another or passionately defending our beliefs. This is how we learn, how we sharpen and correct our thinking, and how we help others to improve. The Holy Spirit often uses the emotional upheaval that accompanies disagreement and conflict to get our attention and drive us to make necessary changes in our families, churches, and personal lives. Conflict can help us to discover our character weaknesses, correct mistaken theological ideas, sharpen our beliefs, refine our plans, grow in wisdom and life experience, learn to trust God during difficult times, and deepen our prayer lives.

3/20/21 What is wrong is for believers to behave in an ungodly, unbiblical manner in the midst of their disagreements. Sadly, such behavior is not uncommon. I have talked to many people who have experienced an agonizing church split. Often what was most upsetting was not the disagreement but the nasty politics that accompanied it—the mean words expressed, the angry attitudes and childish behaviors, the awful displays of pride and selfishness, the backbiting, the minimizing of sin and outright disobedience to God's Word, and the lack of forgiveness or interest in reconciliation.

So when I learned about a fifty-year-old church with a remarkable history of unity and peace, I wanted to know their secret. The church had made a number of difficult doctrinal and stylistic changes during its history. Most of its leaders had strong personalities and had taken decisive action. Yet the church had survived without tearing itself to pieces.

How had this church achieved such unity and made significant changes without a split? The answer of one of the leaders to this very question is key: *"We have always tried by the Holy Spirit's help to think and to act according to biblical principles, especially during our most difficult periods of conflict."*

This church had problems and disagreements like any other

3

church. The people had hurt and irritated one another plenty of times. They knew each other's annoying faults and weaknesses. But they also knew that Christ had called them to love one another fervently, to be humble servants, to submit one to another, to patiently bear with one another, to speak truthfully, to forgive and reconcile their differences, to have right attitudes toward one another, and to display the fruit of the Spirit at all times—especially during times of conflict.

The people of this church knew that "the works of the flesh"—pride, anger, jealousy, and selfish ambition—can destroy a church family and its leadership. They knew that there is a righteous way and a sinful way to treat one another when facing disagreement. They knew that God had provided guidance for handling conflict the right way. So they chose to become people of principle—to follow the specific biblical principles that instruct us in how to deal with conflict. This commitment to biblical attitudes and behaviors governed their responses to one another when conflict arose.

My intent through this book is to explore God's way of handling conflict so that other congregations may also experience peace and unity. This study will draw out from Scripture key principles for handling conflict *with special emphasis on biblical attitudes and behaviors.* Some of these principles are direct statements regarding conflict (Matt.18:15-17). Other principles are derived from general instructions concerning proper Christian behavior that become even more important when Christians are in conflict.

All Christian believers need to know and practice these biblical principles because we all face controversies and relational disagreements. Church leaders especially need to understand the biblical principles for dealing with conflict because leaders greatly influence how conflict is managed in a local church. Leaders at any level can make matters worse when they mismanage conflict. Leaders can also achieve peaceful solutions and just reconciliation when they manage conflict constructively. Churches would help themselves significantly by teaching Christian people how to behave biblically when conflict strikes and by holding one another accountable for sinful behaviors and attitudes. Faithful adherence to biblical principles is the best policy when it comes to preventing damaged relationships and discrediting the witness of the gospel.

My aim for this book is to provide a better understanding of what the Bible teaches about conflict and to help believers learn how to respond to conflict according to biblical principles. In order not to present an overwhelming amount of information, the book focuses strictly on the presentation and exposition of scriptural passages that address conflict in the New Testament churches. It does not deal with practical principles of mediation or arbitration because there are many excellent resources that deal with these subjects. The manageable size and easy-to-remember outline of this book make it a helpful resource for anyone who is dealing with conflict and for church leaders who are teaching God's truth about handling conflict. The first three chapters lay down the foundational biblical principles:

1. Act in the Spirit
2. Act in Love
3. Act in Humility

The remaining seven chapters deal with specific principles for handling conflict:

4. Control the Anger
5. Control the Tongue
6. Control the Criticism
7. Pursue Reconciliation
8. Pursue Peace
9. Face False Teachers
10. Face Controversy

It is imperative that church leaders teach these principles and that all believers practice them. If, when conflict flares, we would simply stop for a moment to reconsider the instruction in God's Word and to seek the Holy Spirit's guidance, we would avoid many of the destructive behaviors that characterize our conflicts. We would prevent unnecessary breaches of fellowship.

One evangelist who had started a number of churches over a forty-year period told me that every one of them eventually folded because of sinful infighting among believers. No deliberate effort had been made to teach the new churches and their leaders how to deal with conflict according to biblical principles. In contrast, a missionary who served elsewhere told me how he and other missionaries worked together to achieve unity among themselves and their organizations. As a result, they saw greater fruit in the gospel.

The country in which this second group of missionaries worked had seen much division among previous missionaries and missions organizations. They wanted to avoid this regrettable situation, so they decided to study why previous Christian missions had failed. They discovered that years of sinful infighting and mistrust between the different missionaries and mission organizations had held back the Lord's blessing and the advancement of the gospel message.

To start afresh, this new group of missionaries drew up a document outlining biblical principles for dealing with conflicts that might arise between them. The document included a pledge to speak the truth to one another and never to slander or backbite. They promised to not gossip about one another and agreed to represent each other's beliefs accurately. They decided to follow scriptural instructions and confront one another about known problems. They committed themselves to pray for one another and to love one another despite their differences. This approach proved tremendously successful.

My heartfelt desire and prayer is that this book will raise fresh awareness among individual believers and churches regarding the importance of teaching, learning, and practicing Christ-honoring principles for handling conflict.

Behold, how good and pleasant it is when brothers
dwell in unity.
Psalm 133:1

If you would like to use this book for individual or group study, a free study guide is provided online at www.lewisandroth.org.
You can also find other important supplementary materials in the "downloads" section of the website.

1

Act in the Spirit

But if you bite and devour one another, watch out that you are not
consumed by one another.
Galatians 5:15

Chapel Hill Church, a large, Bible-believing church, invited an evangelist
for a week of special messages. At the end of the week, the evangelist
challenged the congregation to develop a deeper devotion to Christ and
to be more committed to sharing the gospel. Then—without showiness,
coercion, or endless appeals—he invited people to come to the front of
the auditorium and kneel with him in prayer. His messages had touched
many people's hearts and they responded to his invitation.

But this church was not accustomed to altar calls, and as the
meeting ended a prominent church member expressed to all within
earshot his disagreement with the evangelist's altar call. His loud, angry
words and facial expressions shocked those around him. He accused
the evangelist of unscriptural practices and emotional manipulation.
He even threatened to leave the church if the leadership did not deal
immediately with the situation.

Upon hearing the angry man's accusations, some people jumped
to defend the evangelist. They saw that God had used the evangelist
to revive their spiritually dry church and supported his challenge to
greater evangelism. They accused those who opposed the altar call of
being narrow-minded traditionalists who always resisted change. They
also accused them of being insensitive to the Holy Spirit's leading and
of not caring for the lost.

Other people sided with the angry complainer, claiming that
the evangelist was preaching a gospel of easy-believism. They made
slanderous remarks about the evangelist's motives and character and
labeled anyone who agreed with him as "liberal." They also attacked
the church leaders, saying that they lacked spiritual discernment. They
went so far as to ask the church leadership to resign, claiming that they

had "sinned" against the church by inviting a wolf in sheep's clothing to preach.

Soon gossip and rumors lit up the phone lines. Past grievances against one another were rekindled, and hurtful accusations flew in every direction. Angry, inflammatory speech became the mode of communication. Misinformation, fear, suspicion, and distrust abounded. Friends and family members were recruited to choose sides. The church leadership communicated poorly with the congregation and the anger and hatred escalated.

Within a year, Chapel Hill Church split into two separate groups. Each group claimed to be defending God's truth. There was no desire on the part of either group to seek reconciliation. They were happy to be done with one another.

Although the name Chapel Hill Church and this account are both fictional, the behavior attributed to this church is not. The description of the fight at Chapel Hill Church is not an exaggeration. It reflects the attitudes and behaviors seen in countless other church fights and splits.

Regardless of our theological view of altar calls, we should be able to agree that the behavior of these Christian believers showed total disregard for nearly every biblical command concerning Christian conduct and speech. They behaved like people who knew nothing of the gospel and the Holy Spirit. They acted more like spoiled, ill-mannered children than mature, Spirit-indwelt believers.

Seeing the disastrous effects of such conflicts should compel us to ask, "How are Bible-believing Christians who are indwelt by God's Spirit and in possession of the guidance of God's Word to handle their disagreements?" No group of people should be as well equipped to handle conflict as Bible-believing Christians. The Bible provides detailed instructions for handling conflict constructively. Christ provides the power of the Holy Spirit to enable us to obey God's Word and to control our sinful passions.

The theme of this chapter is foundational to the rest of the book: *When conflict arises, our attitudes and behaviors should reflect our new life in Christ given by the Holy Spirit who lives within us. We are to display the fruit of the Spirit and not the works of the flesh. We are to walk in step with the Spirit's leading. We are to be Spirit-controlled and not flesh-controlled or out of control.* Let us examine this foundational principle as it is expressed in Galatians 5:13-26; 1 Corinthians 3:1-4; and James 3:13-18. These three passages of Scripture form the bedrock upon which much of this book rests. The next two chapters address love and humility, two preeminent fruits of the Spirit.

1. WHEN FACING CONFLICT, DO NOT DISPLAY "THE WORKS OF THE FLESH"

Much of the contentious infighting and unnecessary divisions that plague many churches today result from believers acting according to the flesh and not walking by the Spirit. This was true of some of the New Testament churches as well. Recognizing the potential harm of such behavior, Paul, the apostle, addressed the problem in his letters to the churches of Galatia and Corinth.

> When conflict arises, our attitudes and behaviors should reflect our new life in Christ given by the Holy Spirit who lives within us.

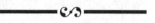

a. Sinful Conflict in the Churches of Galatia

Serious discord over the role of the Mosaic Law in regard to salvation and Christian living threatened the life and unity of the newly planted churches of Galatia.[1] So Paul, one of the founders of these churches, warned the new believers:

> But if you bite and devour one another, watch out that you are not consumed by one another. (Gal. 5:15)

Their conduct, writes one commentator, was "more fitting to wild animals than to brothers in Christ."[2] If these new Christian believers did not stop fighting, no one would survive the carnage.

After Paul warns of the potential for mutual destruction within

---

[1] Acts 13:13-14:27.
[2] R. A. Cole, *The Epistle of Paul to the Galatians*, TNTC (Grand Rapids: Eerdmans, 1965), 157.

the believing community, he identifies the cause as "the works of the flesh":[3]

> Now the works of the flesh are evident: sexual immorality, impurity, sensuality, idolatry, sorcery, *enmity, strife, jealousy, fits of anger, rivalries, dissensions, divisions, envy,* drunkenness, orgies, and things like these. (Galatians 5:19-21; italics added)

The eight social sins italicized above describe sinful attitudes and behaviors displayed among the Galatian believers. It is likely that you have seen many of these behaviors displayed in your own church experience. As you consider these eight "works of the flesh," know this: The Holy Spirit is absolutely opposed to each of them.[4] Verse 17 states, "For the desires of the flesh are against the Spirit, and the desires of the Spirit are against the flesh, for these are opposed to each other." The Holy Spirit does not lead believers to commit these social sins: to bite and devour one another or to provoke one another to fits of anger or bitter jealousy.

Paul also warns that conceit (or pride) is at the root of many of these base, sinful behaviors:

> Let us not become conceited, provoking one another, envying one another. (Gal. 5:26)

Conceit led some of the Galatians to arrogantly provoke others into angry, theological debates in order to prove their superior knowledge. In other cases, conceit led believers to envy those who threatened their self-importance. So instead of "through love [serving] one another" as brothers and sisters in Christ (Gal. 5:13), the Galatians were provoking and envying one another.

Paul's catalog of social vices stands as an objective check to our behavior. So the next time you are involved in conflict, stop and think.

---

[3] The term *flesh* here describes the weak, fallen human condition apart from the life of God and subject to the power of sin. See special note on the word *flesh* in the Appendix.

[4] You can find a detailed explanation of each of the works of the flesh in the "online resources" section of www.lewisandroth.org.

You know you are yielding to "the desires of the flesh" if any of the above sinful vices are displayed in your behavior or attitude.

When the brother in our opening story about Chapel Hill Church spewed out angry accusations against the evangelist, for example, he obviously was yielding to "the desires of the flesh" rather than to the Spirit's leading. When other believers started to divide into contending factions and to feel hostility toward one another, they were displaying rivalry and enmity. These sinful works of the flesh showed clearly that they were not yielding to "the desires of the Spirit."

b. Sinful Conflict in the Church at Corinth

Christians in the church at Corinth also exhibited the sinful "works of the flesh" and experienced disruptive conflict. In fact, "there was not another church founded by Paul, as far as we know, that was so plagued by sin and division."[5] The Corinthian believers had the Holy Spirit, yet in behavior and attitude were like people who are devoid of the Spirit. David Garland comments that they acted "no differently from the rest of Corinthian society."[6] In other words, they were a worldly minded group of Christians.

In his letter to this strife-torn church, Paul puts his finger on the problem:

> . . . you are still of the flesh. For while there is jealousy and strife among you, are you not of the flesh and behaving only in a human way? For when one says, "I follow Paul," and another, "I follow Apollos," are you not being merely human? (1 Cor. 3:3-4)

Although the Corinthians prided themselves on their spirituality and knowledge, their quarrels, jealousies, and factiousness proved that they were not walking by the Spirit. They possessed abundant gifts of the Spirit but lacked the graces of the Spirit. Their manner of life was inconsistent with that of people who profess to walk by the Spirit and represent the truths of the gospel.

---

[5]Ralph P. Martin, *2 Corinthians*, WBC (Waco, TX: Word, 1986), 464.
[6]David E. Garland, *1 Corinthians*, BECNT (Grand Rapids: Baker, 2003), 110.

———— ❧ ————

Works of the Flesh

Enmity	Quarreling
Strife	Jealousy
Jealousy	Anger
Fits of Anger	Hostility
Rivalries	Slander
Dissensions	Gossip
Divisions	Conceit
Envy	Disorder
(Galatians 5:19-21)	(2 Corinthians 12:20)

———— ❧ ————

So in 2 Corinthians 12:20, Paul lists eight sins of discord among the Corinthians that, if continued, would require severe apostolic discipline: "quarreling, jealousy, anger, hostility, slander, gossip, conceit, and disorder." This list of eight social sins is similar to the list in Galatians 5:19-21. All these social sins are evidence of "the works of the flesh" that result in much conflict. There could be no hope for unity in the church at Corinth until believers acknowledged and repented of their fleshly, unChristlike conduct.

2. WHEN FACING CONFLICT, DISPLAY "THE FRUIT OF THE SPIRIT"

God has always wanted his people to live in a way that would demonstrate his holy character to the unbelieving world. As people who are born of God's Spirit, each believer is a "new creation" in Christ (Gal. 6:15) who is to handle conflict in a radically different way from that of the flesh-driven world.[7] *The one thing Christian believers are not to do when engaged in conflict is to revert back to our old, pre-conversion, flesh-driven ways of behavior.*[8]

a. Walk by the Spirit

The Christian life begins the moment a person receives the Holy Spirit of God and experiences a profound, radical life transformation. The difference between the old life before conversion and the new life after conversion is analogous to the difference between death and life or between living in light and living in utter darkness.[9] This new life is to be continued by means of faith in God's Word and dependence on the empowering presence of the Holy Spirit.

Paul assumes that his Galatian readers have believed the gospel and have been born again by the Spirit. However, he reproves them for not living consistently by the Spirit's power and direction. Many of them

---

[7]Lev. 18:1-5; 2 Cor. 6:14-7:1; James 1:27; 4:4.
[8]Eph. 2:1-2; 4:17-29; 5:3-17; Col. 3:7; 1 Peter 1:14; 4:3-4.
[9]*Death and Life*: Rom. 6:13; 1 John 3:14; 5:12. *Light and Darkness*: Eph. 5:8; 1 Peter 2:9.

were trying to live the Christian life in their own strength by following the Old Testament laws of Moses rather than living by the power of the Spirit. Therefore, his response to the interpersonal conflicts and erroneous views of Christian living among the Galatian believers was to tell them to "walk by the Spirit," that is, to be "led by" or "live by" the Spirit:

> But I say, walk by the Spirit, and you will not gratify the desires of the flesh. . . . But if you are led by the Spirit, you are not under the law. . . . If we live by the Spirit, let us also walk by the Spirit. (Gal. 5:16, 18, 25)

This passage is one of the most significant passages in the New Testament for instruction on how to live the Christian life. It is, as one theologian says, "theological dynamite."[10] Walking by the Spirit requires an active, step-by-step, daily effort to live the Christian life by means of the presence and enabling power of the Holy Spirit. *Nothing but the indwelling presence of the Holy Spirit is sufficient to enable believers to resist the desires of the flesh and to live the Christlike life.*

b. Display Christlike Character by the Fruit of the Spirit

The Holy Spirit seeks to form Christlike character qualities in the life of every individual Christian and every local church body. These Christlike qualities promote right attitudes, godly conduct, and healthy human relationships—the very qualities the strife-torn congregations in Galatia desperately needed. Paul's nine descriptions of "the fruit of the Spirit" form a composite picture of Christlike character and conduct: "love, joy, peace, patience, kindness, goodness, faithfulness, gentleness, self-control; against such things there is no law" (Gal. 5:22-23). We know that we are walking by the Spirit when we see "the fruit of the Spirit" displayed in our daily conduct and inner attitudes.[11]

One commentator writes that this fruit is "nothing less than the practical reproduction of the character (and therefore the conduct) of Christ

---

[10]George T. Montague, *The Holy Spirit: Growth of a Biblical Tradition* (New York: Paulist Press, 1976), 200.
[11]You can find a detailed explanation of each of the fruits of the Spirit in the "online resources" section of www.lewisandroth.org.

14

in [the] lives of his people."[12] "The fruit of the Spirit," then, provides an objective guide to our attitudes and behavior when dealing with conflict. So we should always ask ourselves: "Am I displaying Christlike character and the life of the Spirit when I deal with disagreement or someone who opposes me?" Hopefully we should be able to answer: "Yes!" "It is tragic," states Donald Guthrie, "that church life has often been wrecked through failure to observe the responsibilities of walking in the Spirit."[13]

> **Nothing but the indwelling presence of the Holy Spirit is sufficient to enable believers to resist the desires of the flesh and to live the Christlike life.**

When caught in a storm of conflict, one fruit of the Spirit that is especially needed to navigate safely through the storm is "self-control" (Gal. 5:23). *Lack of self-control is a major problem during conflict, but the Holy Spirit provides power over the fleshly excesses generated by the passions of anger, jealousy, hatred, and the spirit of revenge.* Christian believers who control their emotions and thinking by the power of the Spirit are best able to handle conflict constructively and bring about a just resolution. They are Christians who don't bite and devour their brothers and sisters in Christ.

In contrast, when people act according to the flesh, they are out-of-control emotionally. They do not display the fruit of the Spirit and have the potential to do terrible damage to other people and to the name of Christ. Such was the case at Chapel Hill Church. Outsiders would never know that the Spirit of the living Christ dwelt in the hearts of the people there. The people at Chapel Hill Church did not walk in a manner worthy of the gospel, nor did they appear to be new creations in Christ. Instead, anger, pride, revenge, and slander characterized the believers at Chapel Hill Church. It was only a matter of time before they would all be "consumed by one another."

3. WHEN FACING CONFLICT, DISPLAY "THE WISDOM FROM ABOVE"

James, our Lord's half-brother, gives sound advice regarding conflict

---

[12]F. F. Bruce, *The Epistle to the Galatians: A Commentary on the Greek Text*, NIGTC (Grand Rapids: Eerdmans, 1982), 257.
[13]Donald Guthrie, *Galatians*, NCB (London: Oliphants, 1969), 142.

———— ☙ ————

Fruit of the Spirit	**Wisdom From Above**
Love	Pure
Joy	Peaceable
Peace	Gentle
Patience	Open to Reason
Kindness	Full of Mercy
Goodness	Full of Good Fruits
Faithfulness	Impartial
Gentleness	Sincere
Self-Control	
(Galatians 5:22-23)	(James 3:17)

———— ☙ ————

among Christian believers. He writes about two kinds of wisdom that are particularly important to recognize when dealing with conflict:

> But if you have bitter jealousy and selfish ambition in your
> hearts, do not boast and be false to the truth. This is not
> the wisdom that comes down from above, but is earthly,
> unspiritual, demonic. For where jealousy and selfish ambition
> exist, there will be disorder and every vile practice. But the
> wisdom from above is first pure, then peaceable, gentle, open
> to reason, full of mercy and good fruits, impartial and sincere.
> (James 3:14-17)

First there is "the wisdom from above," which is from God's Spirit. It produces purity of heart and mind, sweet reasonableness, graciousness, mercy, sincerity, and peace (James 3:17). Then there is the wisdom from below, which "is earthly, unspiritual, demonic." It produces uncontrolled speech, bitter jealousy,[14] selfish ambition, unbridled passions, strife, pride, "disorder and every vile practice" (James 3:2-4:6).

When we experience heated disagreements with fellow Christians, we should use James 3 to guide our conduct and speech because it directly addresses controlling the fiery tongue and defines proper Christian conduct. Without such wisdom, we are at great risk to "bite and devour one another."

In one church, for example, some people jumped to their feet to high-five one another, hoot, and rejoice immediately after the congregation narrowly and contentiously voted to fire the pastor. They didn't seem to care that the pastor's children stood nearby, looking on as people celebrated the ousting of their father from his position. What impact do you think such behavior had on their view of Christian people and life in the church?

How does God view such behavior? We only have to read James 3:15 to learn that such behavior reflects the wisdom from below and "is earthly, unspiritual, demonic." Such behavior produces "disorder and

---

[14]Take note that jealousy (or envy) is prominent in all the vice lists. Jealousy is a major cause of conflict between Christians and especially between churches and ministers of the gospel (Phil. 1:15; Rom. 13:13; Gal. 5:20, 21, 26; 1 Cor. 3:3; 2 Cor. 12:20; James 3:14, 16). Love, however, "does not envy" (1 Cor. 13:4).

every vile practice" within the church family. The winners may have won their election and ousted the pastor, but at the judgment seat of Christ, God will have the last word on their "success."[15]

4. LEARNING TO HANDLE DISAGREEMENT AS A SPIRIT-CONTROLLED CHRISTIAN

Conflict presents one of the toughest challenges to walking by the Spirit. If only we would recognize that every conflict is a test as to whether or not we will display Christlike character, the wisdom from above, and the reality of the gospel in our lives.[16] If only the believers who ousted their pastor had recognized the test and sought to conform their attitudes to the wisdom from above. If only the believers at Chapel Hill Church had recognized the test and been as concerned about their sinful attitudes and conduct as they were about altar calls. Incredibly, believers in both cases were willing to act sinfully and unbiblically in order to "win" or prove themselves "right." They did not seem to care that they were grieving the Holy Spirit of God by acting according to "the works of the flesh," which the New Testament clearly denounces.

In many church disputes, believers fight for so-called truths that are not explicitly revealed in Scripture while egregiously violating the clear and repeated teaching of Scripture on godly conduct and attitudes. This chapter began, for example, with the story of the brother who made an angry outburst after an evangelist's altar call. He, and the members and leaders of Chapel Hill Church, displayed "the works of the flesh" rather than "the fruit of the Spirit" as they dealt with the issue. What could they have done differently to keep in step with the Spirit and the instructions of our Lord Jesus Christ?

a. Pray

As soon as the man realized that he was emotionally upset, he should have asked his heavenly Father for wisdom and self-control. If he had

---

[15] 1 Cor. 3:12-17; 2 Cor. 5:10.
[16] Deut. 13:3; 1 Cor. 11:19.

prayed "in the Spirit,"[17] the Holy Spirit would have brought to mind specific scriptural passages—ones he had read many times—about how a Spirit-led believer thinks and acts when emotionally upset. In fact, all the members of Chapel Hill Church needed to pray for the Spirit's guidance before taking action.

Prayer is essential to walking by the Spirit. Through prayer, the Holy Spirit convicts us of our sin and moves us to confess and amend our ways. The sinful attitudes and behaviors of people on both sides indicate that they did not sincerely trust God's instructions or the Spirit's power. Rather, the angry man and the other members of the church took matters into their own hands, ultimately letting their flesh dictate their behavior.

b. Check Our Attitudes and Conduct

God does not lead his people to "bite and devour one another" like wild animals. As well-taught Christians, the angry brother and other members of Chapel Hill should have *checked their attitudes and conduct by the rule of God's Word which the Spirit always uses to direct the Lord's people.* They should have recognized that they were yielding to "the desires of the flesh" and displaying "the works of the flesh" and the wisdom from below. They should have recognized that anger was rising up and vying for control and that they must exercise extra caution in order to prevent uncontrolled anger from becoming a golden opportunity for the devil to do his destructive work (Eph. 4:27).

They needed to renounce all gossip and slander against the evangelist and inflammatory accusations against one another. These behaviors could not be justified by the excuse that they were fighting for the truth because their behavior contradicted the truth. They had lost all balanced perspective on what is most important. Altar calls are not inherently sinful; what *is* sinful is giving free reign to unrestrained anger and hostility toward others. Everyone involved needed to wait until their emotions subsided and their minds cleared so that they could address the issue with Spirit-directed wisdom, patience, gentleness, reasonableness, and self-control.

---

[17]Rom. 8:26-27; Gal. 4:6; Eph. 6:18; Jude 20.

c. Act in Love

Love would have moved the man to think first of the spiritual welfare of the people around him rather than his personal desire to make known his opinion and vent his anger. A loving, Christlike attitude would have said: "I don't personally agree with altar calls, but I know that this evangelist preaches Christ crucified to many lost people. For that I thank God. I will get down on my knees and pray that the Spirit will use him to see many more people come to Christ."[18]

Putting the welfare of others first is what it means to walk in love by the power of the Spirit. Instead, the believers of Chapel Hill Church did not act in love toward one another. They did not bear "with one another in love" (Eph. 4:2). They had knowledge of love (of which they were very proud!) but violated every New Testament principle of love.

d. Seek the Counsel of Spirit-filled Believers

Before the man condemned all altar calls, he should have sought the counsel of the church leaders. Scripture states that the Holy Spirit sets "overseers" in the flock to shepherd "the church of God" (Acts 20:28). The man did not consult with the church shepherds to express his concerns or to ask for their guidance. In fact, the church leaders should have invited people to talk with them if they had questions or had heard rumors that needed to be addressed.

Seeking counsel from other Spirit-filled believers is one way of being led by the Spirit. The people needed their leaders to remind them of proper Christian attitudes and behavior during stressful times of disagreement. They needed their leaders to warn them about the divisive sins of gossip and slander. It is unfortunate that the church leaders failed to quickly acknowledge the problem and to present to the congregation a clear, constructive course of action (see Acts 6:1-3).

---

[18]This attitude emulates Paul's example: "The former proclaim Christ out of rivalry, not sincerely but thinking to afflict me in my imprisonment. What then? Only that in every way, whether in pretense or in truth, Christ is proclaimed, and in that I rejoice" (Phil. 1:17-18).

e. Treat Others with Kindness and Gentleness

The man who had a problem with the evangelist didn't seem to know the appropriate attitudes or manner by which to handle controversy among his fellow believers. Yet 2 Timothy 2:24-26 is quite clear:

> And the Lord's servant must not be quarrelsome but kind to everyone, able to teach, patiently enduring evil, correcting his opponents with gentleness. God may perhaps grant them repentance leading to a knowledge of the truth, and they may escape from the snare of the devil, after being captured by him to do his will.

Although the above passage applies directly to dealing with false teachers and their followers, it also serves as a guide for how we should treat fellow believers with whom we have doctrinal disagreement.

When the time was right, the man could have approached the evangelist and, without making accusations or attacking his motives, gently asked about his reasons for altar calls. He may have learned something from the evangelist; on the other hand, he may also have helped the evangelist. Perhaps both of them would have learned more of what it means to walk in a manner "worthy of the gospel of Christ" (Phil. 1:27).

f. Be Humble

After evaluating his behavior and seeing the chaos he caused in the church, the man needed to humble himself and repent of his angry outburst. He had chosen the wrong time and place to speak out. He had slandered and questioned the motives of a fellow servant of the Lord, which he had no right to do. He needed to recognize his sin and repent, and he needed to apologize to the people who had heard his angry accusations.

When sinful infighting broke out, the leaders of the church should have called for prayer, fasting, and repentance in order to restore an attitude of humility and love. They should not have tried to deal with the problem until self-serving, sinful attitudes were first amended.

With an attitude of Spirit-controlled humility, the disagreement over altar calls could have been handled civilly and constructively. Instead, believers chose to bite and devour one another and make a first-class display of "the works of the flesh."

How will we respond to conflict as individual believers and within our church families? Will we display the beautiful fruit of the Holy Spirit, or will we display the ugliness of the flesh? Every conflict reveals whether we practice what we preach, whether we are doers of the Word or hearers only (James 1:22). Every conflict reveals the genuineness of our Christian life (1 Cor. 11:19). Jesus said, "If you know these things, blessed are you if you do them" (John 13:17) and we each are accountable to him.

If we live by the Spirit, let us also walk by the Spirit. Let us not become conceited, provoking one another, envying one another.
Galatians 5:25-26

Key Principles to Remember

1. When facing conflict, display "the fruit of the Spirit," not "the works of the flesh." Be Spirit controlled, not out of control.

2. Be as concerned about your attitude and behavior as about the issue of disagreement.

3. Do not "bite and devour one another."

2

Act in Love

Love covers a multitude of sins.
1 Peter 4:8

The issue of conflict among believers was of deep concern to Francis Schaeffer, one of the most influential evangelical thinkers and writers during the last half of the twentieth century.[1] Schaeffer is perhaps best known for opening his home in the Swiss Alps (called L'Abri, which is French for "the shelter") to anyone seeking answers to life's ultimate questions. *Time* magazine described his "mission to intellectuals" as "one of the most unusual missions in the Western world."[2]

As a young college student and new Christian, Schaeffer realized that his home church and denomination had abandoned historic, orthodox Christianity for theological liberalism, so he left his denomination to become part of a newly formed evangelical denomination. Within two years, however, personality and doctrinal issues led the new denomination to split into two groups. Schaeffer became an active participant in the minority group that formed its own denomination and seminary. Years later, he voluntarily left that denomination. It went through a division shortly afterward.

Francis Schaeffer knew from hard, personal experience the ugliness that can occur among true believers in the midst of doctrinal differences. It grieved him to see people bite and devour one another in the name of Christ. He saw that something was seriously wrong with the way Christians handled their disagreements and concluded that *the missing element was love.*[3]

Believers, Schaeffer taught, are to be known not only for their uncompromising stand for the truth of Scripture but also for their

---

[1]For a biography, see Colin Duriez, *Francis Schaeffer: An Authentic Life* (Wheaton, IL: Crossway, 2008).
[2]"Mission to Intellectuals," *Time* (January 11, 1960).
[3]Duriez, *Francis Schaeffer: An Authentic Life*, 87. Francis Schaeffer, *The Church Before the Watching World*, in *The Complete Works*, Vol. 4, Book 2 (Westchester, IL: Crossway, 1983), 151-63.

unwavering love for one another—even when they disagree. Fighting for truth, right doctrine, and the purity of the church must be balanced with love and grace. To speak the truth and to act in love *simultaneously*, to use Schaeffer's terminology, requires the empowering work of the Holy Spirit. Balancing truth and love cannot be done in the flesh.[4]

1. LOVE DEFINES HOW TO ACT WHEN FACING CONFLICT

Schaeffer's teaching about acting in love when standing for truth is not new. Paul was a tireless defender of the truth of the gospel, yet he wrote more about love and conflict than any other New Testament writer. Love and truth are not enemies, nor does one need to be sacrificed for the other. Love, in fact, "rejoices with the truth" (1 Cor. 13:6).

Paul's insistence on practicing love in the midst of conflict is evident in his dealings with the church in Corinth. Although the Corinthians prided themselves on their knowledge and giftedness, they were infamous for their contentiousness and infighting. They lacked love and consequently were tearing the church down, not building it up; they were dividing the church, not uniting it; they were subverting God's work, not enhancing it.

> Believers are to be known not only for their uncompromising stand for the truth of Scripture but also for their unwavering love for one another—even when they disagree.
>
> ———— ✧ ————

Paul writes to the Corinthians that love is indispensable to all that they do and say (1 Cor. 13:1-3) and follows up with fifteen specific descriptions of love (vv. 4-7). Christians today often view these verses as a love poem and recite them in marriage ceremonies, but this was not Paul's intent. *Paul was writing to a church in conflict, and we must understand his message in that context:*

---

[4]"We must look moment by moment to the work of Christ, to the work of the Holy Spirit. Spirituality begins to have real meaning in our moment-by-moment lives as we begin to exhibit simultaneously the holiness of God and the love of God" (Schaeffer, *The Church Before the Watching World*, 152).

Love is patient and kind;
love does not envy or boast;
it is not arrogant or rude.
It does not insist on its own way;
it is not irritable or resentful;
it does not rejoice at wrongdoing, but rejoices with the truth.
Love bears all things, believes all things, hopes all things,
endures all things. (1 Cor. 13:4-7)

After listing two positive qualities of love ("patient" and "kind"), Paul lists eight vices that are totally incompatible with love. Each of these vices expresses sinful self-centeredness that creates and exacerbates conflict and tears apart relationships. These sins are the work of the flesh; they dominated the church in Corinth, and they continue to generate conflict in churches and in the personal lives of Christians today.

When we demand our way and our selfish desires are frustrated, we fight and quarrel. Notice how James describes the workings of our selfish desires:

What causes quarrels and what causes fights among you? Is it not this, that your passions are at war within you? You desire and do not have, so you murder. You covet and cannot obtain, so you fight and quarrel. (James 4:1-2)

Genuine Christian love, in contrast, is not preoccupied with self, is not puffed up with pride, is not easily provoked to anger, and does not hold grudges or seek revenge (1 Cor. 13:4-5). Christian love is displayed in the love of Jesus who "laid down his life for us," as an example that "we ought to lay down our lives for the brothers" (1 John 3:16).

Many of the first Christian churches brought together people from such distinct and diverse social classes that conflict was inevitable. Slaves and free, rich and poor, educated and uneducated, and traditional Jews and permissive Gentiles found that they were no longer separated by their social status but were united as brothers and sisters in Christ. How could such a congregation possibly hold together? Only through the self-sacrificing love produced by the Holy Spirit! As one commentator states, "it is this love (and only this love) which is strong enough to hold together a congregation of disparate individuals."[5]

So don't be caught off guard. When we face conflict, Paul's instructions on love from 1 Corinthians 13:4-7 *define how we should and should not behave.*[6] Before a potentially explosive meeting or a tense, personal confrontation, review in your mind the biblical descriptions of love. Remember that love is the first fruit of the Holy Spirit,[7] so choose to "walk in love" (Eph. 5:2) by the power of the Spirit. Remind yourself of how love does and doesn't act. *Decide beforehand how you should respond toward those with whom you disagree.* Don't let love be the missing element in your relationships with your brothers and sisters in Christ.

2. LOVE DOES NOT SEEK REVENGE FOR WRONGS SUFFERED

Even today, some primitive, tribal groups practice a custom called "spearing." The custom requires the tribe of a person who is wounded or killed by someone from another tribe to spear someone from the offending tribe in revenge. To not exact revenge for harm done to one's own tribal member would bring shame; to forgive would be considered weakness. These unwritten laws perpetuate endless tribal warfare and senseless killing.

Christians in conflict today don't literally throw spears at each other, but we do plenty of "spearing" with cutting words and angry looks. In contrast, *Jesus taught and lived by the principle of nonretaliation.* "If anyone slaps you on the right cheek," he said, "turn to him the other also" (Matt. 5:39). In his commentary on 1 Peter, Thomas R. Schreiner describes Jesus' silence in suffering as "the most remarkable evidence of his nonretaliatory spirit since the urge for revenge can be almost

---

[5]James D. G. Dunn, *The Epistles to the Colossians and to Philemon*, NIGTC (Grand Rapids: Eerdmans, 1996), 232.
[6]For an exposition of each of these fifteen qualities, see Alexander Strauch, *A Christian Leader's Guide to Leading With Love* (Littleton, CO: Lewis and Roth, 2006), 39-88.
[7]Rom. 5:5; 15:30; Gal. 5:22; Col. 1:8.

unbearable when mistreatment takes place."[8]

Following Jesus' teaching and example, Paul and Peter prohibit the get-even mentality that is so much a part of human nature:

- Repay no one evil for evil. (Rom. 12:17)

- Do not repay evil for evil or reviling for reviling, but on the contrary, bless, for to this you were called. (1 Peter 3:9)

- When he was reviled, he did not revile in return; when he suffered, he did not threaten, but continued entrusting himself to him who judges justly. (1 Peter 2:23)

When someone insults us, we are not to return the insult; when cursed, we are not to curse back; when someone strikes us, we are not to strike back; when treated maliciously, we are not to retaliate. We are to be different from those who do us evil.[9] Instead of returning evil for evil, we are to walk in love and not become like our enemies or those with whom we fight.

Love desires to reconcile and repair relationships. It leaves past injustices in God's hands. Thus the Scripture forbids personal vengeance or taking justice into our own hands: "Never avenge yourselves, but leave it to the wrath of God, for it is written, 'Vengeance is mine, I will repay, says the Lord'" (Rom. 12:19). It is God's prerogative to punish evil, and he has given authority to human government and courts to judge and punish evildoers (Rom. 13:1-7).

Love is not "resentful" (1 Cor. 13:5), meaning it does not keep a record of wrongs in order to get even. Love does not nurse grudges or pick at old wounds. It does not dwell obsessively on grievances. In short, *love lowers the temperature of most conflicts by refusing to engage in retaliation*. Love is not overcome by evil but overcomes evil with good (Rom. 12:21). It offers forgiveness to the offender and asks for forgiveness when needed.

Paul and Barnabas are two giants of the faith who disagreed

---

[8]Thomas R. Schreiner, *1, 2 Peter, Jude*, NAC (Nashville, TN: Broadman & Holman, 2003), 143.
[9]Lev. 19:17-18; Prov. 20:22; 24:17-18, 29.

with one another sharply. They provide an important biblical example of how Christian believers disagree without seeking revenge or carrying on a lifetime of bitter warfare. When they had a "sharp disagreement" over whether to take John Mark, Barnabas' cousin, on their second missionary journey, they went separate ways. Barnabas took Mark, Paul took Silas, and they formed two separate evangelistic teams (Acts 15:36-41).

Luke's account leaves the dispute between Paul and Barnabas unresolved. Even the best of God's servants can disagree with one another and may find that they cannot work intimately together. However, although their disagreement was sharp, Paul and Barnabas didn't carry on years of personal warfare against each other. They didn't send out letters attacking each other's character. They didn't form new denominations. Instead, they refused to speak evil of one another or to keep records of frustrations and wrongs. In fact, Paul later spoke well of Barnabas as his partner in the gospel (1 Cor. 9:3-6) and even requested that Mark join him because, as he wrote to Timothy, "he is very useful to me for ministry" (2 Tim. 4:11; also Col. 4:10).

3. LOVE OVERCOMES EVIL THROUGH PRAYER, FORBEARANCE, AND KINDNESS

The world loves the sweet music of revenge, but God loves the sweet music of prayer, forbearance, and kindness. So when we are hurt or treated unjustly, we are to handle the conflict with Godlike forbearance and Christlike kindness.[10] We do this first by seeking God's help and guidance in prayer, then by displaying loving forbearance and kindness through our behavior.

a. Prayer

In a culture where hatred for one's enemies and seeking personal revenge

---

[10]*Patience*: Ex. 34:6; Jer. 15:15; Rom. 2:4; 9:22; Gal. 5:22; 1 Tim. 1:16; 2 Peter 3:9, 15. *Kindness*: Ruth 2:20; 2 Sam. 9:3; Ps. 106:7; 145:17; Luke 6:35; Rom. 2:4; 11:22; Eph. 2:7; Titus 3:4; 1 Peter 2:3. *Paul's example and instructions*: 2 Cor. 6:3-4, 6; 2 Tim. 2:24; 4:2.

were not only acceptable practices but refined art forms, Jesus' radical statements on love must have shocked his followers:

- Love your enemies and pray for those who persecute you. (Matt. 5:44)

- Love your enemies, do good to those who hate you, bless those who curse you, pray for those who abuse you. (Luke 6:27-28)

When people, whether they are believers or nonbelievers, abuse or persecute us, we are to respond with the most positive, proactive display of love possible. Jesus does not call us to be passive martyrs who merely grin and bear it; we are to actively "bless" those who wrong us and not "curse" them (Rom. 12:14; 1 Peter 3:9)! Our Lord wants us to pray that God would have mercy on and change the hearts of those who persecute and abuse us.[11] *Such prayer is a key element in dealing with conflict in a God-honoring way.*

Love lowers the temperature of most conflicts by refusing to engage in retaliation.

When we pray for those who wrong us, the Holy Spirit transforms our character, making us more like Christ. The Spirit directs our hearts in how to respond with love and also works in the hearts of those for whom we pray. But when we neglect to pray, *we leave God out of our conflicts and operate independently of his guidance and power.*

b. Forbearance

In this life, we will suffer many hurts and injustices, even from friends and relatives. When Christians are wronged, we are to respond in love. In fact, the first quality of love listed in 1 Corinthians 13:4-7 is patience, which can also be translated "longsuffering" or "forbearance." When we patiently endure the injuries and wrongs suffered in the midst of conflict, we demonstrate this tenacious quality of love. In contrast, crying over every hurt or slight is often an expression of our self-centeredness and self-pity.

---

[11]Luke 23:34; Acts 7:60.

Scripture informs us that one of the chief ways to maintain "the unity of the Spirit in the bond of peace" is by "bearing with one another in love" (Eph. 4:2-3). The little prepositional phrase, "in love," is very important. If we don't forbear "in love," our forbearance "could result in resentment or anger rather than love."[12]

Forbearance as opposed to impatience, which focuses on self and will create or exacerbate conflict, deals with other people carefully in a patient, self-controlled manner that is conducive to resolving conflict constructively. The Christian virtue of forbearance enables a believer to practice the love that "covers a multitude of sins" (1 Peter 4:8).

> When we neglect to pray, we leave God out of our conflicts and operate independently of his guidance and power.

When we are tempted to be impatient with others, we should stop and think for a moment of the gracious longsuffering of God with our many wrongs against Him. As Paul reminds us: "bearing with one another and, if one has a complaint against another, forgiving each other; as the Lord has forgiven you, so you must also forgive" (Col. 3:13). In light of God's patience toward us, who are we to think that we cannot patiently bear with the weaknesses and failures of others, or the wrongs they do to us?

c. Kindness

Instead of being "overcome by evil" when we are wronged, the Bible teaches us to respond with deeds of kindness (1 Cor. 13:4). Showing kindness demonstrates that we are walking by the Spirit and walking in love even when we are under the emotional stress of interpersonal conflict. So in the context of love (Rom. 12:9-21), Paul writes that we are to *overcome* evil with good deeds of kindness:

> If your enemy is hungry, feed him; if he is thirsty, give him something to drink; for by so doing you will heap burning coals on his head. Do not be overcome by evil, but overcome evil with good. (Rom. 12:20-21)

---

[12]Harold W. Hoehner, *Ephesians* (Grand Rapids: Baker, 2002), 510.

As believers, we are to win people with kindness. With all sincerity of heart, we are to bless those who abuse us by doing good deeds for their benefit. By deeds of kindness, we demonstrate that we are prepared to forgive those who have sinned against us. May it be said of us as it was said of Thomas Cranmer, an archbishop of the Church of England: "To do him any wrong was to beget a kindness from him."[13]

Paul could say to the Corinthians that his life and ministry were marked by patience, kindness, love, and power of the Holy Spirit:

> We put no obstacle in anyone's way, so that no fault may be found with our ministry, but as servants of God we commend ourselves in every way . . . [by] patience, kindness, the Holy Spirit, genuine love. (2 Cor. 6:3-4, 6).

If you would like others to treat you with patience and kindness when engaged in conflict, then treat those who disagree with you with patience and kindness. This is the Golden Rule of love: "So whatever you wish that others would do to you, do also to them, for this is the Law and the Prophets" (Matt. 7:12).

4. LOVE COVERS A MULTITUDE OF SINS

After one Sunday morning service, I saw a man approaching me. The special music had been a little loud that morning and from the look on his face I knew what was coming. He angrily told me that I would face the judgment of Christ for allowing the young people to ruin his worship! For several minutes he gave me a good, old-fashioned tongue-lashing. He held nothing back.

Then he took a deep breath, rested for a few seconds, and said calmly, "Well, at least you are an open-minded person." He turned, walked away, and there has been no problem between us since.

I never said a word. I knew that if I started to argue, the situation would have escalated. Surely the Holy Spirit controlled my emotions, allowing me to stay calm and to overlook his threatening talk and ungracious behavior.

---

[13]Alfred Tennyson, *Queen Mary* (Boston, MA: James R. Osgood, 1875), 194.

At times such behavior has to be confronted and rebuked, but sometimes the best thing to do is to say nothing and choose to overlook a person's fault. In this case, because I knew the person well, the wisest course of action was not to pursue the matter or to demand that he apologize. The right course of action was to follow Peter's plea: "Above all, keep loving one another earnestly, since love covers a multitude of sins" (1 Peter 4:8). Love for this brother allowed me to understand his deeply felt perspective on worship and to bear with his character weaknesses. Love, and only love, covers a multitude of sins.

In the church, just as in the secular world, we often have to deal with difficult people. Every person is sinful and imperfect. We all have eccentricities and character flaws. If we do not, "above all," bear with one another in love and allow love to cover our offenses, we cannot live in unity. Only Spirit-produced love gives us the power to understand people's weaknesses and problems, and to repeatedly forgive, or to cover, one another's faults. Jesus' love for his disciples covered their many failures and allowed him to live and work with them.

Although love covers a multitude of sins, we must remember that it does not cover all sins. As Ken Sande, the author of *The Peacemaker*, explains:

> To truly overlook an offense means to deliberately decide not to talk about it, dwell on it, or let it grow into pent-up bitterness. If you cannot let go of an offense in this way, if it is too serious to overlook, or if it continues as part of a pattern in the other person's life, then you will need to go and talk to the other person about it in a loving and constructive manner.[14]

At times, love requires the church's discipline of sin—perhaps even severe action or words to stop a destructive situation—to preserve the welfare of the person and to protect the local church.[15] The purpose of such discipline is not to expose and shame, but to correct, redeem, and restore. Genuine love exercised in "the wisdom from above," however, recognizes when to expose and when to cover an offense. Genuine love

---

[14]Ken Sande, *The Peacemaker: A Biblical Guide to Resolving Personal Conflict*, 3rd ed., (Grand Rapids: Baker, 2004), 83.
[15]Matt. 5:22-24; 18:15-17; 2 Cor. 2:2-4; 7:8-13; Gal. 2:11-14; 2 Thess. 3:6-15.

does not bite and devour; it always seeks the good of the other person over one's own vindication.

5. LOVE DENIES SELF FOR THE GOOD OF OTHERS

A number of young Christian couples from the same church went on a ski retreat. Some of the couples brought wine to have with the evening meal. A few of the couples did not want to drink, but the wine drinkers insisted that there was nothing wrong with drinking wine during a meal. They convinced the nondrinkers to join them and not to be so rigid.

Later, however, the nondrinkers felt that they had violated their consciences. They became upset with those who had pressured them to drink, and those who pressured them brushed aside the nondrinkers as being legalistic and ignorant. This caused a rift in their relationships. It led to disputes within the church about who was right and who was wrong.

> The foundation of Christian ethics is not freedom or rights but costly, self-sacrificing love that builds up the Lord's people.

Such disputes are nothing new or unusual. In most of the first-century churches, disputes arose over issues of conscience and opinions about lifestyle choices.[16] In Rome, for example, Jewish and Gentile Christians fought over food regulations and the observance of holy days (Rom. 14). Christians today argue and divide over questions of Sabbath keeping, celebrating Christmas, drinking alcohol, or enjoying certain types of entertainment and music.

Among the various principles the Bible lays down for resolving disputes, love is foremost. Love, the Bible tells us, "does not insist on its own way" (1 Cor. 13:5) and "does no wrong to a neighbor" (Rom. 13:10). Love is even prepared to die for a brother or sister (1 John 3:16).

In keeping with this teaching, Paul describes in Romans 14:1-15:9 how to walk in love and put the spiritual welfare of others before our own rights and liberties:

---

[16]In Romans 14:1, Paul refers to these controversial issues as "opinions," or "disputed matters" (NIV). By this he means they are not fundamental doctrines but secondary matters of personal conscience. See chapter 6 for more detail on this subject.

For if your brother is grieved by what you eat [the issue in dispute at that time], you are no longer walking in love. By what you eat, do not destroy the one for whom Christ died. (Rom. 14:15)

In a similar vein, he addresses the abuse of Christian liberty that was taking place in the churches of Galatia:

For you were called to freedom, brothers. Only do not use your freedom as an opportunity for the flesh, *but through love serve one another.* (Gal. 5:13; italics added)

For Paul, freedom in Christ meant loving, slave-like service to others,[17] not self-indulgence. It is the flesh—always preoccupied with the self and ready for a fight—that demands its rights and freedoms. Exercising his "rights" was not Paul's chief concern. The guiding principles that governed his actions were building up believers in their faith, winning the lost to Christ, and glorifying God in all things (1 Cor. 10:24, 31-33).

The foundation of Christian ethics is not freedom or rights but costly, self-sacrificing love that builds up, rather than tears down, the Lord's people. If we apply the principle of love to the disagreement over drinking wine, Christlike love requires that the couples who are free to drink wine not pressure the nondrinkers to drink or to mock them for their views. Christlike love would have put the alcohol aside so that it would not become an issue that would break the fellowship between brothers and sisters in the Lord.

For the nondrinkers, it would be a sin to go against their conscience (Rom. 14:23). However, even while they chose to abstain, the nondrinkers could choose to encourage the others to enjoy their liberty. Of course, if any in the group struggled with alcoholism, drinking wine in front of him or her would be a thoughtless display of selfishness.

When matters of personal conscience and lifestyle choices become an issue, *the New Testament remedy is a costly love—a love that radically and voluntarily surrenders one's rights and freedoms for the spiritual*

---

[17]John 13:14; Rom. 15:1-3, 8; 1 Cor. 8:1, 13; 9:19-23; 10:24, 32-33; Gal. 5:13; 6:2.

edification of others. To practice liberty-limiting love is to imitate Christ's self-sacrificing love on the cross for our salvation. "For Christ did not please himself" (Rom. 15:3). If Christ was willing to die for the weak believer, surely we can give up some of our freedoms and rights to build up and protect such a person from stumbling into sin.

6. PRACTICE WHAT YOU PREACH ABOUT LOVE

Obedience to Jesus' "new commandment" to love one another as he loved us (John 13:34-35) is the best protection against much senseless conflict. The problem is, while it is easy to talk about love, it is hard to practice what we preach when emotionally charged, anger-inducing conflict arises. Recognizing this problem, the beloved disciple John writes, "Little children, let us not love in word or talk but in deed and in truth" (1 John 3:18). Love is of little help in handling conflict if it is not "genuine" or if it is not practiced (Rom. 12:9).

An experience that my friend Brian shared with me illustrates how important it is (and how difficult it can be) to practice what we preach. Brian owns a computer business and had worked for several months to set up a computer system for a business. When the job was complete, the customer said he couldn't pay for it. Brian described the customer as one of the most difficult people—unreasonable, argumentative, and mean-spirited—he had ever dealt with in business. He dreaded even talking to him on the phone.

> But what good is it to preach that God the Father's love is *in* and *among* us if we fight like the devil?

When Brian called the customer to insist that he start paying something on his debt, the man threatened to pay him nothing! During their conversation Brian asked, "What is your business, anyway?"

The man replied, "It's a conflict management organization."

Brian couldn't believe his ears! Astonished by the man's hypocrisy, he was too shocked to reply and too bewildered to laugh at the irony of it. Later, when Brian attempted to set up a payment plan, the customer threatened to refuse to speak to him again. At that point, Brian asked, "Couldn't we use some of the principles you teach about conflict management to resolve our issue in a reasonable way?"

The customer angrily repeated his threats. It took more than a year for my friend to be paid, but as a result of his patient, self-controlled conduct and speech, the two parties ended their relationship on a positive note.

Just as the man who taught conflict management did not practice what he preached, we Christians sometimes fail to practice the glorious principles of divine love that we preach. But what good is it to preach that God the Father's love is *in* and *among* us (John 17:26) if we fight like the devil? What good is it to preach that "love does no wrong to a neighbor" (Rom. 13:10) if we seek to destroy our neighbor with whom we disagree? What good is it to preach that the first fruit of the Holy Spirit is love if we display hostility and hate? What good is it to preach the "new commandment" to love one another as Jesus loved us if we fight like dirty politicians who have no integrity or concern for their opponents?

Most of us have at least a general idea of proper Christian behavior, but in the heat of the moment when our emotions are stirred up, we revert to unloving, ungodly behaviors—fits of anger, inflammatory speech, prideful self-justification. We even press lawsuits and seek personal revenge. So the crucial question is always: Will we act in love, even under the stress of conflict, or will we act like people who are devoid of the Holy Spirit and the love of God?

"It is not what one knows," remarks Peter Davids, "but what one does that counts. True knowledge is the prelude to action, and it is the obedience to the Word that counts in the end."[18] Through prayer, the Holy Spirit's enabling power, the guidance of God's Word, and our commitment to the truths of the gospel, we can (and must) learn to act in love at all times.

An ancient story about John, the beloved disciple, illustrates the importance of love in the believing community. John lived to be nearly one hundred years old. Jerome, a fourth-century biblical scholar, records that John became so feeble in his old age that his disciples had to carry him into the congregational meetings. Although he could no longer preach and his speech was difficult to understand, John repeatedly said,

---

[18]Peter H. Davids, *James*, NIBC (Peabody, MA: Hendrickson, 1989), 41.

"Little children, love one another." Wondering why he always said the same thing, one of his disciples asked, "Teacher, why do you always say this?" To this question the aged John replied, "Because it is the Lord's commandment, and if it alone is done, it is enough."[19]

If you know these things, blessed are you if you do them.
John 13:17

Key Principles to Remember

1. When facing conflict, practice what you preach about love.

2. Practice the principle of nonretaliation.

3. Overcome the hurts of conflict with prayer, forbearance, and positive deeds of kindness.

4. Be prepared to surrender your rights and freedoms in Christ for the spiritual edification of others.

---

[19]Jerome, *Commentarius ad Galatas* (6:10). Patrologia Latina (Patrologiae cursus completus, series latina), vol. 26, edited by J.-P. Migne (Paris 1866), column 462C. English translation by Michael Woodward.

3

Act in Humility

Christ Jesus . . . did not count equality with God a thing to be grasped,
but . . . humbled himself.
Philippians 2:5-6, 8

The first-century church in the city of Philippi (northeast Greece today)
brought immense joy to Paul's heart. It was a mature, doctrinally sound
church with overseers, deacons, and industrious workers for the gospel.
The Philippian believers had become Paul's beloved friends, and they
financially supported his ministry more than any other New Testament
church. Yet even this model church was not immune to pride, selfish
ambition, complaining, and infighting.

When conflict arose within the congregation, Paul knew that it
must be dealt with swiftly and properly or more serious problems would
arise. The Philippians were not yet biting and devouring one another,
but that would soon follow if the contention continued. "The seeds of
dissension had been sown," remarks Moisés Silva, "and they were not to
be allowed to sprout."[1] So Paul, one of the church founders, passionately
appeals for unity:

> Complete my joy by being of the same mind, having the same
> love, being in full accord and of one mind. (Phil. 2:2)

Paul's emotional plea for like-mindedness, mutual love,
harmony of spirit, and oneness of purpose is equally important for
churches today. Without unity, churches will be destroyed by infighting
and their witness in the world will be lost. How does a church achieve
this "full circle of unity—from one mind, to one love, to one spirit,
to one purpose"?[2] The answer is Christlike humility: "Have this mind
among yourselves, which is yours in Christ Jesus" (Phil. 2:5).

---

[1]Moisés Silva, *Philippians*, WEC (Chicago, IL: Moody, 1988), 102.
[2]John MacArthur, *Philippians* (Chicago, IL: Moody, 2001), 109.

1. DENOUNCING WRONG ATTITUDES IN THE CHURCH

Sinful attitudes fuel conflict and make matters worse, so managing conflict constructively and biblically begins with the right attitudes.[3] *It is important for church leaders to promote Christlike attitudes within the church, which is precisely what Paul does in his letter to the Philippians.* He forcefully denounces selfish ambition and conceit and charges believers to follow Christ's example of humility and selfless service to others:

> Do nothing from rivalry or conceit, but in humility count others more significant than yourselves. Let each of you look not only to his own interests, but also to the interests of others. (Phil. 2:3-4)

This is one of the most significant New Testament directives on relating to one another when engaged in conflict. When Christ's attitude of humble servanthood permeates a local church, it can weather any storm. But when pride characterizes a church body, every little disagreement stirs up a whirlwind. Even something as insignificant as changing the color of a Sunday school room can divide such a group. For this reason, Paul admonishes everyone in the church to: "Do nothing from rivalry or conceit." Let us examine these twin instigators of discord and division.

When Christ's attitude of humble servanthood permeates a local church, it can weather any storm.

— ☙ —

a. Selfish Ambition

If unity of mind was to be achieved in the church at Philippi, rivalry among some prominent members had to be recognized as a divisive work of the flesh and stopped. The word "rivalry" in Philippians 2:3

---

[3]Malcolm Cronk states: "With the right spirit, a clumsy church structure will work. Without the right spirit, an ideal structure won't work." Quoted by Marshall Shelley in *Well-Intentioned Dragons* (Minneapolis, MN: Bethany, 1994), 81.

could be better translated as "selfish ambition,"[4] meaning "selfish devotion to one's own interests"[5] without regard for the interests of others or the cost to others. Selfish ambition is self-centered, contentious, competitive, and factious.

In the strongest language possible, James states that selfish ambition "is earthly, unspiritual, demonic." It leads to "disorder and every vile practice" and causes "quarrels" and "fights" (James 3:15-16; 4:1-3). It "stands at the heart of human fallenness," writes Gordon Fee, "where self-interest and self-aggrandizement at the expense of others primarily dictate values and behavior."[6]

Selfish ambition, particularly on the part of those in leadership, has plagued the world throughout human history. It is one of five "global giants"—hunger, sickness, illiteracy, spiritual emptiness, and selfish leadership—that one Christian philanthropist has identified as essential to deal with in order to help the poor.[7] "Selfish leadership" is evident in the "me first" philosophy of some government officials who rule by greed and lust for power. Such leaders care little about social justice or the needs of the people. To them, a position of authority is merely a means of enriching themselves and lording their authority over people.

As deplorable as it is, this problem also plagues churches. Self-seeking, controlling leaders look out for their own interests rather than the interests of those they are called to serve, like Diotrephes in the first century, who liked to put himself first (3 John 9-10). Leaders like Diotrephes make Christian ministry "all about me." In stark contrast, Paul—a model of Christlike servant-leadership—tells the Corinthians,

---

[4]The Greek word *eritheia* is difficult to translate precisely. Although the ESV renders it "rivalry" in Philippians 2:3, many translations and commentators prefer here the rendering "selfish ambition." The idea of *selfishness* fits the context of Philippians 2:2-8 better. The ESV does use "selfish ambition" in translating *eritheia* in James 3:14, 16. The Greek term is also used in other of our key passages: Gal. 5:20; 2 Cor. 12:20; Phil. 1:17. See Friedrich Buchsel, "*eritheia*," in *Theological Dictionary of the New Testament* (Grand Rapids: Eerdmans, 1964), 2: 661.
[5]Richard N. Longnecker, *Galatians*, WBC (Dallas, TX: Word, 1990), 256.
[6]Gordon D. Fee, *Paul's Letter to the Philippians*, NICNT (Grand Rapids: Eerdmans, 1995), 186.
[7]David Van Biema, "The Global Ambition of Rick Warren," *Time* (August 18, 2008), 40.

"For what we proclaim is not ourselves, but Jesus Christ as Lord, with ourselves as your servants for Jesus' sake" (2 Cor. 4:5). He goes on to say, "So death is at work in us, but life in you" and "I seek not what is yours but you. . . . I will most gladly spend and be spent for your souls (2 Cor. 4:12; 12:14-15).

Selfish ambition also caused conflict among Jesus' disciples. James and John asked Jesus for the top positions in his kingdom: "Grant us to sit, one at your right hand and one at your left, in your glory" (Mark 10:37). This request sparked rivalry among the other disciples who "began to be indignant at James and John" (Mark 10:41). They became indignant because they, too, desired power and glory for themselves! The question of who was the greatest became a matter of debate among the Twelve and a cause of consternation for our Lord.

When Paul was imprisoned in Rome, some Christian preachers, motivated by jealousy and selfish ambition, even preached the gospel in Rome in an attempt to add to Paul's misery during his imprisonment (Phil. 1:15, 17). Thus Paul knew from personal experience the ugliness and pain of this particular sin. He hated to see the same attitudes creeping in to his beloved church at Philippi.

Selfish ambition has no place in the family of God! It is utterly incompatible with our blessed Lord's teaching on humble servanthood and brotherhood.[8] It is antithetical to Christlike, sacrificial love.

Selfish ambition is not a fruit of the Spirit; it is a work of the flesh. It undermines people who are trying to work together in unity. It motivates people to be demanding and controlling and to brush aside anyone who disagrees with them. Only those who have the spirit of Christlike humility can handle positions of power and authority without oppressing others or serving and exalting self. So heed the words of the Spirit of the Lord: *Do nothing from selfish ambition.*

b. Conceit or Pride

The church in Philippi delighted Paul's heart,[9] but Satan would not allow this blessed condition to continue unchallenged. His intent was to divide and conquer, and there is hardly a better way to spoil an

---

[8] Matt. 20:26; 23:8, 11-12; Mark 9:35; 10:43; Luke 22:26; John 13:4-15; 13:34-35.
[9] Phil. 1:3-8; 2:25-30; 4:1, 10, 14-18.

exemplary church than through pride in doctrinal correctness, giftedness, generosity, or success! Satan knows that "Pride goes before destruction, and a haughty spirit before a fall."[10] So provoking people's pride, especially the pride of "rightness," is an effective scheme for corrupting a good church. "Making an idol out of doctrinal accuracy, ministry success, or moral rectitude," writes Timothy Keller, "leads to constant internal conflict, arrogance and self-righteousness, and oppression of those whose views differ."[11]

Paul was painfully aware of what was happening among certain prominent persons in the church. He saw that, like its companion selfish ambition, conceit was igniting conflict and spoiling unity. So he admonished the believers to do nothing from conceit, which is literally "empty glory."[12]

Conceit, or pride, gives us a distorted view of reality. It deceives us into thinking that we are better than others, that we know a lot more than we really do, or that we are more holy or gifted than we actually are. "Nothing is higher than lowliness of mind," writes John Chrysostom, "and nothing is lower than boastfulness."[13] Because the nature of pride is to think too highly of oneself, Paul warns:

• I say to everyone among you not to think of himself more highly than he ought to think, but to think with sober judgment. (Rom. 12:3)

• For if anyone thinks he is something, when he is nothing, he deceives himself. (Gal. 6:3)

Conceit produces vain boasting and feelings of superiority that hinder conflict resolution. Conceit causes us to be defensive, self-righteous, and stubborn. It blinds us to our own errors and glaring faults. It keeps

---

[10]Prov. 16:18; see also 1 Tim. 3:6; 1 Chron. 21:1-8.

[11]Timothy Keller, *Counterfeit Gods: The Empty Promises of Money, Sex, and Power, and the Only Hope That Matters* (New York: Dutton, 2009), 132.

[12]Conceit, the noun *kenodoxia*, denotes "a vain or exaggerated self-evaluation" (BDAG, 538). The Greek adjective *kenodoxos* is used in Galatians 5:26, where it is closely associated with envy and provocation: "Let us not become conceited, provoking one another, envying one another."

[13]Chrysostom, *Homilies on the Gospel of Saint Matthew*, 65.5, NPNF, 1ˢᵗ Series, 10:402.

us from listening to wise correction or rebuke, and from learning and changing.

During the past four decades, I have talked to many people who have left abusive churches that were led by harsh, extremist leaders. These believers are often confused as they sort through their experience in search of their true faith. As we talk, I often ask what was so appealing about being a member of such an extreme sect and why they remained so long under the influence of an abusive leader. They invariably identify the heart of the problem as pride: pride in their superior understanding of doctrine, pride in their achievement of a higher spirituality, pride in being one of the few who are more enlightened. They say that before they left these churches, they would have preferred to die than to admit that they were wrong. Pride had blinded them to the truth that their church was missing many of the fruits of the Spirit such as genuine love for all believers and true humility of mind.

Pride was a problem in nearly every church in the New Testament period,[14] and it is still a problem. Pentecostal and charismatic churches boast of their supernatural power and higher spiritual life while patronizing those who do not share their experiences. Churches of the Reformed tradition look down on those who do not accept their polished systematic theology. Lutherans hold themselves aloof because of their reformation heritage, doctrinal distinctives, and hero of the faith, Martin Luther. Baptists take pride in their large numbers and democratic church policies. Some churches are so proud of their holy, separate living that they refuse even to fellowship with other believers whom they critically judge to be worldly, defiled compromisers.

Even if one were to be completely correct in all doctrine and practice, there is still no room for pride. Pride displeases God. It is the first of the seven deadly sins God hates (Prov. 6:16-19). When Christians have an attitude of superiority and show contempt for their brothers and sisters in the Lord, they are not walking by the Spirit; they are yielding to fleshly pride. The result is bound to be relational conflict.

The verdict on pride is clear: "Pride only breeds quarrels" (Prov. 13:10 NIV). Since no human—even the most godly, devoted believer—is exempt from the internal struggle with pride, the Bible directs every

---

[14]Rom. 11:20, 25; 12:16; 1 Cor. 1:30; 4:8; 8:1-2; 12:21; 13:2; 2 Cor. 12:7-11; Phil. 2:3.

believer to dress with the clothes of humility and act humbly toward all fellow believers,

> Clothe yourselves, *all of you, with humility toward one another*, for "God opposes the proud and gives grace to the humble." (1 Peter 5:5; italics added)

C. S. Lewis describes pride as "spiritual cancer: it eats up the very possibility of love, or contentment, or even common sense."[15] If we, like the Philippians, are to stop fighting and maintain the love and unity of the Spirit, we must come before God honestly and deal with our perverse, stubborn pride. We must humble ourselves before God, acknowledge our empty conceit, and repent of it. "Smooth relations in the church can be preserved," writes Thomas Schreiner, "if the entire congregation adorns itself with humility. . . . Humility is the oil that allows relationships in the church to run smoothly and lovingly."[16] Humility is essential to unity and peace in the local church.

2. TEACHING RIGHT ATTITUDES IN THE CHURCH

How tragic that after years of ministry, a missionary would confide to his close friend that his biggest frustration has been a lack of humility among believers that has caused nearly continual fights and divisions. A lack of humility prompted Andrew Murray, the beloved devotional writer and missionary statesman from South Africa, to write:

> When I look back on my own religious experience, or on the Church of Christ in the world, I stand amazed at the thought of how little humility is sought after as the distinguishing feature of the discipleship of Jesus. In preaching and living, in the daily activities of the home and social life, in the more special fellowship with Christians, in the direction and

---

[15]C. S. Lewis, *Christian Behavior* (London: Centenary, 1943), 43.
[16]Thomas R. Schreiner, *1, 2 Peter, Jude*, NAC (Nashville, TN: Broadman & Holman, 2003), 238.

performance of work for Christ—how much proof there is that humility is not esteemed the cardinal value.[17]

a. Understanding Christlike Humility and Servanthood

And yet, the biblical remedy for the attitudes of selfish ambition and vain conceit that lead to conflict and contentious relationships in the body of Christ is nothing less than humility. Paul's message in Philippians 2:3-5 is crystal clear:

> "Making an idol out of doctrinal accuracy, ministry success, or moral rectitude leads to constant internal conflict, arrogance and self-righteousness, and oppression of those whose views differ."
> —Timothy Keller

In humility count others more significant than yourselves. Let each of you look not only to his own interests, but also to the interests of others. Have this mind among yourselves, which is yours in Christ Jesus.

The Greek word translated as humility literally means "lowliness of mind," or "humble-mindedness."[18] Humility is "the grace of 'lowliness,'"[19] the virtue of modesty that considers others "more significant than" ourselves. The humble person sees himself or herself in right perspective before an infinite, perfect, glorious creator-redeemer God and as a servant to others.

Counting others "more significant than yourselves" means not being preoccupied with ourselves and our needs. It means that we serve others, put their needs ahead of our own, promote their advancement, and bear one another's burdens.[20]

Unity is best accomplished among those who have a humble mind and a servant heart. If we are to avoid conflict in our churches and handle it properly when it occurs, we must be humble, Christ-centered people, not those who are concerned with our own self-

---

[17]Andrew Murray, *Humility* (Springdale, PA: Whitaker, 1982), 7.
[18]"Humility" (*tapeinophrosynē*) is a compound word made up of the two words "lowly" (*tapeinos*) and "mind" (*phrosynē*).
[19]Peter T. O'Brien, *Colossians, Philemon*, WBC (Waco, TX: Word, 1982), 200.
[20]See Rom. 15:1-3; 1 Cor. 10:24; 13:5; Gal. 5:13-14; 6:2.

centered ego. "Unity is impossible," writes one commentator, "if each is out for himself, each promoting his own cause, each is seeking his own advantage."[21] Gordon Fee aptly makes the point:

> Here is the road to true unity among believers. . . . If "selfish ambition and vain glory" are sure bets to erode relationships within the church, then the surest safeguard to a healthy church is when "considering each other as more important than oneself" characterizes its people, especially those in positions of leadership.[22]

b. Taking on the Attitude of Christ

To drive home with unforgettable force his exhortation to take on the humble mind of Christ, Paul turns to the supreme example of Christ's humility and self-sacrifice displayed by his incarnation and death on the cross:

> Have this mind among yourselves, which is yours in Christ Jesus, who, though he was in the form of God, did not count equality with God a thing to be grasped, but made himself nothing, taking the form of a servant, being born in the likeness of men. And being found in human form, he humbled himself by becoming obedient to the point of death, even death on a cross. (Phil. 2:5-8)

"Unity is impossible if each is out for himself, each promoting his own cause, each is seeking his own advantage."
—Gerald F. Hawthorne

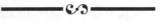

There is no more powerful statement in all of Scripture than this: "he humbled himself by becoming obedient to the point of death, even death on a cross."

Jesus Christ is no grasping, self-absorbed, egocentric deity! He gave himself totally for the sake of others. He left the glories of heaven and came to earth to die upon the cross for the salvation of sinners.

---

[21]Gerald F. Hawthorne, *Philippians*, WBC (Waco, TX: Word, 1983), 68.
[22]Gordon D. Fee, *Paul's Letter to the Philippians*, NICNT (Grand Rapids: Eerdmans, 1995), 189.

Commenting on Paul's description of the profound significance of Christ's example of humility, Paul Rees writes:

> "Don't forget," cries Paul, "that in all this wide universe and in all the dim reaches of history there has never been such a demonstration of self-effacing humility as when the Son of God in sheer grace descended to this errant planet! Remember that never—never in a million aeons—would He have done it if He were the kind of Deity who looks 'only to his own interests' and closes His eyes to the 'interests of others!' You must remember, my brethren, that through your union with Him, in living, redemptive experience, this principle and passion by which He was moved must become the principle and passion by which you are moved."[23]

Only when we begin to comprehend the full extent of what the self-emptying Christ has done for us will we be motivated to imitate his humility in all our relationships, especially when we are involved in conflict with our brothers and sisters in Christ. But to have such humility, we must keep the cross before us every day. In the shadow of the cross there is no room for sinful pride and selfish ambition. *How can we be proud when Christ was humble? How can we selfishly serve ourselves when he unselfishly served others?* Or, as one notable theologian said, "How can anyone be arrogant when he stands beside the cross?"[24]

> Only when we begin to comprehend the full extent of what the self-emptying Christ has done for us will we be motivated to imitate his humility.

Jesus dramatically illustrated the humble servant attitude in the upper room before the last Passover meal. As the twelve disciples quarreled about who would be considered the greatest (Luke 22:24), Jesus—their master, teacher, and Lord—knelt down and washed their feet:

---

[23]Paul Stromberg Rees, *The Adequate Man: Paul in Philippians* (Westwood, NJ: Revell, 1959), 43.

[24]The statement is by Carl Henry, quoted by C. J. Mahaney in *Humility: True Greatness* (Sisters, OR: Multnomah, 2005), 68.

He laid aside his outer garments, and taking a towel . . . began to wash the disciples' feet. . . . When he had washed their feet . . . he said to them, "If I then, your Lord and Teacher, have washed your feet, you also ought to wash one another's feet. For I have given you an example, that you also should do just as I have done to you." (John 13:4-5, 12, 14-15)

This is the humble servant attitude that is able to handle disagreement and conflict in a constructive and godly manner.

3. HUMILITY CHANGES A CHURCH

We might wonder what happened when the Philippians read Paul's letter. How did they respond? We know from Polycarp's letter to the Philippians some 50 years later (ca. AD 110-117) that the church was alive and united.[25] They apparently responded appropriately as they had in the past (Phil. 2:12).

Paul intended his letter to be read to the assembled congregation. It is likely that as the Philippian believers heard it, they realized that they were acting proudly and selfishly and were not walking by the Spirit or walking in love. They could certainly see that they had forgotten to exemplify the humble mindset of Christ, and as a result, they were complaining, arguing, and fighting (Phil. 2:14; 4:2-3).

What a rebuke they must have felt as Paul gently redirected their focus away from themselves to the supreme example of Christ's humility, death upon the cross for others, and glorious resurrection. They would have clearly understood that only by copying the attitude of Christ their Lord could they restore unity and joy to the congregation and make their beloved Paul's joy complete "by being of the same mind . . . the same love . . . in full accord and of one mind" (Phil. 2:2).

Even two thousand years later, Paul's description of Christ's self-humbling and self-sacrifice is so moving that we can only imagine how profoundly it must have affected the Philippian believers. We who read Paul's words today also need to humble ourselves, love and serve others,

---

[25]You can read this letter in *The Apostolic Fathers*, edited and translated by Michael W. Holmes (Grand Rapids: Baker, 2007).

break the habit of complaining and arguing, and stop our petty, selfish fighting with one another.

In humility count others more significant than yourselves. Let each of you look not only to his own interests, but also to the interests of others.
Philippians 2:3-4

Key Principles to Remember

1. When facing conflict, check your attitude first.

2. Act and speak with the humility of Christ, "the Philippians 2 attitude."

3. Don't act or speak when motivated by selfish ambition or pride.

4

Control the Anger

*Let every person be . . . slow to anger, for the anger of man does not
produce the righteousness that God requires.*
James 1:19-20

Simeon and Levi, two of Jacob's twelve sons, became enraged when their
sister Dinah was raped by a man named Shechem. Although the brothers'
moral indignation was justified, they responded with unrestrained anger
(Gen. 33:18-34:31). They lied, plundered an entire city, brutally killed
every male of that city, and dishonored God by not seeking his guidance
in determining their response. Jacob later decried their actions, saying,
"Cursed be their anger, for it is fierce, and their wrath, for it is cruel!"
(Gen. 49:7).

Some Christian people today who would never curse, steal, miss
a prayer meeting, or think of getting drunk, respond with unrestrained
anger toward those who disagree with them. Like Simeon and Levi
these Christians overreact, slaying their brothers and sisters in Christ
and plundering the church. They feel perfectly justified in sending hate
mail or in spreading venom via the Internet. But the Holy Spirit stands
in absolute opposition to all such "works of the flesh" (Gal. 5:17) and
loveless behavior (1 Cor. 13:4-7).

*One of the most important biblical principles for handling conflict
constructively is to control the passions of anger.* Most disputes wouldn't
be nearly as unpleasant and unprofitable if people didn't lose control
of their tempers and say harsh and irrational things to one another.
Unrestrained anger creates and escalates conflict. It makes problem
solving and peacemaking far more difficult than it should be. It is
how we most viciously bite and devour one another (Gal. 5:15). The
principles for handling anger in a manner that displays "the fruit of
the Spirit" rather than "the works of the flesh" are plainly laid out in
Scripture: be slow to anger; control expressions of anger; put off the old
and put on the new self.

1. BE SLOW TO ANGER

God is slow to anger, and for that we should be eternally grateful.[1] Furthermore, God expects his children to be like him—as Paul says, to "be imitators of God, as beloved children" (Eph. 5:1)—so we also must be slow to anger.

Proverbs, the Old Testament book of wisdom, praises those who are patient and slow to anger. It values their strength and discipline more highly than that of mighty warriors (Prov. 16:32). It recognizes that whoever is slow to anger "quiets contention" (Prov. 15:18) and "has great understanding" (Prov. 14:29).

In the midst of contention, only those who are slow to anger are able to bring peace. Those who are slow to anger are more rational and objective than quick-tempered people. They possess the calm, cool demeanor that is needed to navigate through the storms of conflict. In contrast to the "calmness" of those who are slow to anger, "a hot-tempered man stirs up strife" (Prov. 15:18). Whereas a person "who has a cool spirit" (Prov. 17:27) will bring understanding to a situation, a hot-tempered person can't handle a disagreement without losing self-control and making an ugly scene.

> Whoever "is slow to anger quiets contention."
> Proverbs 15:18

In keeping with the wisdom of the Old Testament, James provides early Jewish Christian congregations with invaluable instruction for dealing with internal church conflict:

> Let every person be quick to hear, slow to speak, slow to anger, for the anger of man does not produce the righteousness that God requires. (James 1:19-20)

The wise counsel James offers applies to Christians today as well. We are to be careful to listen to what others say, to be slow to speak our mind or express our opinions, and to be slow to express anger. Too often, however, our pattern of behavior is the exact opposite. When we are opposed or frustrated we are quick to express our anger, spout our own

---

[1]Ex. 34:6; Ps. 103:8; Isa. 7:13; Jer. 15:15; Rom. 2:4; 9:22; Gal. 5:22; 1 Tim. 1:16; 2 Peter 3:9, 15.

opinions, defend ourselves, and resist listening to others. Furthermore, we are to be slow to anger because "the anger of man does not produce the righteousness that God requires" (James 1:20). Sinful anger does not produce the kind of righteous, godly behavior that God requires of his children. If we are to please God and wisely deal with conflict in a righteous manner, we must learn to be slow to anger.

2. CONTROL THE PASSIONS OF ANGER

As Bible-believing Christians, we especially need to control our anger when we deal with doctrinal and ethical issues. We often are passionate about our beliefs and can become angry when those beliefs are challenged. *But anger (even for the cause of righteousness and truth) that is not controlled by the Holy Spirit and the principles of God's Word, will destroy God's people and the witness of the gospel.*[2]

> **Anger short-circuits open and fruitful communication and hinders honest discussion of the issues.**

The problem is, anger is like fire. It can be used for heating and cooking or it can burn down the house. When disputes arise and analytical judgment is most needed, anger often flares out of control. It turns reason into irrationality and confusion. It short-circuits open and fruitful communication and hinders honest discussion of the issues.

a. Be Angry, but Do Not Sin

Anger is a normal human emotion that everyone experiences. It also is an emotion that God experiences. His holy anger burns against evil (Ps. 7:11) yet always remains perfectly controlled and just. As God's

---

[2]Long ago Jonathan Edwards observed: "Men are often [accustomed] to plead zeal . . . for the honour of God, as the cause of their indignation, when it is only their own private interest that is concerned. . . . It is remarkable how forward men are to appear, as if they were zealous for God . . . in cases wherein their . . . interest has been touched, and to make pretence of this in injuring others or complaining of them" (*Charity and Its Fruits* [1852; reprint ed., Edinburgh: Banner of Truth, 1978], 198).

children, we should feel the righteous indignation that he feels when we encounter gross injustice or blatant wickedness (Ps. 119:53). Righteous anger should energize us to fight injustice, moral corruption, and false doctrine. Anger over the horrors of the slave trade, for example, drove William Wilberforce to fight for more than forty years to abolish the slave trade in England.[3]

Jesus was never indifferent toward falsehood or sin. Motivated by perfect righteousness, he drove the moneychangers out of God's temple because the religious leaders of Israel had turned God's house of worship into a merchandise mart for their own enrichment. Led by the Holy Spirit, Jesus expressed God's righteous anger toward those who had made the temple "a den of robbers."[4]

The problem for those of us who follow in Jesus' footsteps is that righteous anger can quickly morph into sinful anger.[5] This is why the Scripture says:

Be angry and do not sin. (Eph. 4:26)

Our natural tendency is to sin when we experience anger. We let anger fester and consume us, or we seek to avenge ourselves by any means. We let our anger grow uncontrolled, which plays right into the devil's hands. Victory over such temptation is possible only by walking in step with the leading of the Holy Spirit and the instructions of God's Word.

b. Deal with Anger Promptly, and Do Not Give the Devil a Helping Hand

If we do not handle our anger properly, the frightening reality is that the devil will seize upon our anger as an opportunity to do terrible harm to us personally and to the believing community corporately. Martyn Lloyd-Jones writes, "Nothing, I maintain, so constantly gives the devil

---

[3]Kevin Belmonte, *Hero for Humanity: A Biography of William Wilberforce* (Colorado Springs, CO: NavPress, 2002).
[4]Matt. 21:12-13; cf. John 2:13-17.
[5]"This almost exclusively negative judgment of anger in man explains why the New Testament is so much more restrained in its concessions than the world around" (Gustav Stählin, "*orgē*," in TDNT, 5 [1967]: 421).

an opportunity as loss of control in anger."[6] The devil exploits masterfully the anger of believers to tempt them to sin. He loves nothing more than to stir up angry, shameful disputes among believing churches, families, and friends.

The Scripture, therefore, instructs us to "not let the sun go down on [our] anger, and give no opportunity to the devil" (Eph. 4:26-27). Sinful anger gives the devil an "opportunity" in a believer's life or within a Christian congregation to gain a foothold and accomplish his evil work. To prevent this, all followers of Jesus are to deal with anger promptly and properly so that it will not turn into bitterness and hate (Matt. 5:21-24). One family took the instruction of Ephesians 4:26-27 quite literally. They made it a practice to ask each other before retiring to bed if there were any unresolved issues they needed to discuss in order to prevent anger and bitterness from entering their relationships. This is an example of what it means to "not let the sun go down on your anger." Don't go to sleep until you have faced the situation and dealt with it constructively.

Sadly, many believers are unaware of "the schemes of the devil" (Eph. 6:11) and unwittingly fall into his trap. It takes only one person who is "given to anger" to cause "much transgression" (Prov. 29:22). One Bible-believing denomination, for example, had a major split primarily because of one angry man who relentlessly campaigned against everyone in the denomination who disagreed with him regarding the time of the Lord's return. Years later, this man realized that he had sinned against many by slandering their character and motives. He acknowledged that he had been angry and out of control. His confession was accepted, but the damage could not be undone. Don't be naïve about angry people. One angry person can destroy an entire congregation.

> "Nothing, I maintain, so constantly gives the devil an opportunity as loss of control in anger."
> —Martyn Lloyd-Jones

c. Be Calm, and Do Not Escalate Conflict through Angry Responses

When we face conflict, we not only have to deal with our own anger,

---

[6]D. Martyn Lloyd-Jones, *Darkness and Light; An Exposition of Ephesians 4:17-5:17* (Grand Rapids: Baker, 1982), 234.

we have to control how we respond to the anger of others. The guiding biblical principle for responding to an angry person is found in Proverbs 15:1:

> A soft answer turns away wrath, but a harsh word stirs up anger.

Faithful adherence to this principle helps to defuse tense situations. I have seen it work effectively many times in my own life and ministry.

In most cases, a soft, gentle response to an angry outburst will placate an angry person. So when someone speaks to you in anger or is upset about an issue in the church, consciously and carefully guard your choice of words. When you speak, answer gently. Intentionally lower the volume of your voice and maintain a pleasant tone. Keep your emotions under control. If you do this, the angry person usually will begin to calm down. As the Scripture says, "A soft tongue will break a bone" (Prov. 25:15).

If, however, you raise the volume of your voice or speak harshly in response, you are, in effect, throwing gasoline on a fire. An explosion will most certainly occur. Remember, "fits of anger" and "hostility" are works of the flesh that only make matters worse (Gal. 5:20; 2 Cor. 12:20). Love, however, is "not easily angered" (1 Cor. 13:5 NIV). "A fool gives full vent to his spirit" declares Proverbs (Prov. 29:11). A wise person, in contrast, will hold back in order to "turn away wrath" (Prov. 29:8). In any disagreement a calm and gentle spirit imparts peace, sweet reasonableness, and the wisdom from above.

3. STRIP OFF THE OLD LIFE OF ANGER, PUT ON THE NEW CLOTHES OF CHRISTLIKE CHARACTER

One of the most godly, gracious, and gentle men I have ever met is a missionary to Angola. I was surprised when I heard him openly confess that he had a hot temper when he was a young man. He recognized, however, that his temper displeased the Lord and knew that it would cause serious problems on the mission field. So he determined to make a change in attitude with the help of the Holy Spirit. In biblical terms, he stripped off the old clothes of sinful anger and put on the new garments of Christlike patience, gentleness, and self-control. Indeed, Christian growth in sanctification always involves putting off the "old self" and putting on the "new self" (Col. 3:5-17).

a. Take off the Old Garments

At conversion, believers "put off [the] old self" and "put on the new self" of Christlikeness. Our new life in Christ demands practical lifestyle changes (Eph. 4:22, 24). One of these changes is to banish "all bitterness and wrath and anger and clamor and slander . . . along with all malice" (Eph. 4:31) because these characterize the "old self" that "was crucified with him" (Rom. 6:6). Paul uses the imagery of taking off old clothes and putting on new ones to emphasize the change of heart and character that takes place in a true believer. In practical language, he writes:

> But now you must put them all away: anger, wrath, malice, slander . . . seeing that you have put off the old self with its practices and have put on the new self, which is being renewed in knowledge after the image of its creator. (Col. 3:8-10)

Angry attitudes are part of the old, unregenerate lifestyle that has no place in the wardrobe of a new person in Christ. As new creatures in Christ then, believers must strip off the dirty garments of the old self. We must, as Paul admonishes, put away "all bitterness and wrath and anger and clamor and slander" (Eph. 4:31).

For some people, it isn't easy to take off the old garments of anger, but I'd like to share the story of one man who, through the power of God's Word and the Holy Spirit, found victory over anger:

> As a new Christian, I was challenged to apply my weekly
> Bible study personally. I was working through Colossians. The
> Holy Spirit caught my attention with Colossians 3:8: "But
> now is the time to get rid of anger, rage, malicious behavior,
> slander, and dirty language." I tried to slide past it, but he kept
> bringing me back to the words "get rid of anger."

I had a violent temper. Whenever it flared, I'd haul up and bash my fist into the nearest door. Even though I often bloodied my knuckles and once completely smashed a beautiful diamond and onyx ring my wife had given me, I couldn't seem to stop. Yet here was God's Word: "Get rid of anger." This wasn't just advice given to the people of Colossae centuries ago. It was God speaking to me right then.

So I made a covenant with God to work on controlling anger. My first step was to memorize the verse and review it daily. I prayed and asked the Lord to bring this verse to mind whenever I might be tempted to lose my temper. I also asked my wife to pray for me and remind me of this verse if she saw me failing in my promise to the Lord. So Colossians 3:8 became a part of my life and gradually removed that sin from me.[7]

If you, too, need to put off your old garments of sinful anger, the following time-proven steps will help you.

First, stop and pray immediately when you sense sinful anger arising in your mind and body.

Some situations are so emotionally upsetting and troublesome that you must immediately go to God in prayer for calmness, self-control, and guidance. When you are overwhelmed with fear and anger, you may not want to pray or think of God's Word or the Spirit's leading; you may want to seek revenge and justice on your own terms. It may feel good for a moment to blow off steam and tell people off, but later you will regret your words and actions. If you indulge in sinful anger, you cannot avoid hurting people or dividing a church or family. You will join the club of the angry fools described by Solomon:

- A fool gives full vent to his spirit, but a wise man quietly holds it back. (Prov. 29:11)

---

[7]Leroy Eims. *The Lost Art of Disciple Making.* (Grand Rapids: Zondervan, 1978), 78-79.

- He who has a hasty temper exalts folly. (Prov. 14:29)

- Be not quick in your spirit to become angry, for anger lodges in the bosom of fools. (Eccl. 7:9)

Second, remember that other people are watching how you respond to a provoking situation.

Your public reputation and character are on the line whenever you are provoked. If you act like an angry fool, you will lose the respect of your family, friends, and fellow believers. But if you control your anger and act calmly and reasonably, those who witness your conduct will hold you in greater esteem.

Third, don't speak or act until you have control over your emotions.

Your first duty is to deal with your anger before you speak to others or attempt to solve a problem. Do nothing until you extinguish the flames of anger within you:

> A wise man may indeed experience the heat, but he will do nothing till he cools again. When your clothes outside are on fire you wrap yourself in a blanket, if you can, and so smother the flame: in like manner, when your heart within has caught the fire of anger, your first business is to get the flame extinguished. Thereafter you will be in a better position to form a righteous judgment, and follow a safe course.[8]

If you sense that you can't control your emotions, tell those around you that you are struggling. They will understand. They know the power of anger and how hard it is to control. If they are wise and caring people, they will pray with you. They can help to calm the situation or put matters off to a later time when emotions have cooled down.

---

[8]William Arnot, *Studies in Proverbs* (1884; reprint ed., Grand Rapids: Kregel, 1978), 398.

Fourth, if you do sin in anger, confess your sin and seek forgiveness immediately.

Sinful, out-of-control anger is self-justifying and self-deceiving. Even Christians can do horrible things to others and rationalize their actions in their own minds. So be careful. Trying to justify sinful anger will only make matters worse. If you sin against others with angry, abusive words or with glaring looks, go to them and deal with it quickly. Confess your sin and ask forgiveness of anyone against whom you have sinned.

> "Let all bitterness and wrath and anger and clamor and slander be put away from you, along with all malice."
> Ephesians 4:31

Fifth, if you struggle with anger, avail yourself of the help God provides.

Start by studying what his Word says about anger. The Holy Spirit will use this knowledge to convict, correct, and transform you. He will change your thoughts and motives, helping you to rid yourself of all anger, wrath, clamor, malice, and bitterness.[9] Pray each day for grace to control your temper, and seek godly counsel on anger management through books and other people.

Sixth, avoid associating with angry people.

Some Christians are so prone to anger that Scripture says they are to be avoided:

> Make no friendship with a man given to anger, nor go with a wrathful man, lest you learn his ways and entangle yourself in a snare. (Prov. 22:24-25)

It is easy to imitate bad role models, so pick Christlike role models, and be a good role model yourself. Do not associate with angry people because you may learn their ways and become like them.

---

[9]Eph. 4:31; Col 3:8.

b. Put on New Clothes

Putting off the old clothes of anger is only half the job. It leaves us naked and vulnerable. To finish the job, we must put on new clothes—the virtues and graces of Christ:

> Put on then, as God's chosen ones, holy and beloved, compassion, kindness, humility, meekness, and patience, bearing with one another and, if one has a complaint against another, forgiving each other; as the Lord has forgiven you, so you also must forgive. And above all these put on love, which binds everything together in perfect harmony. (Col. 3:12-14)

In a world full of anger and violence, God does not want his children to be known as militant, angry people. Hot-tempered behavior does not reflect the character of Christ or the work of the Holy Spirit. So we must put on new garments that befit our status as a "new creation" in Christ. *Only when we are properly dressed in Christlike character can we handle conflict properly or discuss reasonably and profitably our doctrinal differences or policy issues.*

If we put on the new clothes of Christlike character, it not only makes a difference in our church conduct, but can touch the hearts of those who are hostile toward the gospel. When a well-known Christian apologist met with a group of college students to answer questions about the Christian faith, one student was particularly antagonistic toward the gospel message. In past meetings he had often provoked Christians into angry debate. Throughout the discussion, this young skeptic did everything in his power to bait the apologist and disrupt the meeting, but the apologist remained calm and responded kindly, patiently, and gently (1 Cor. 13:4; 2 Tim. 2:24-26).

At the end of the evening, impressed by the apologist's gracious demeanor, the young man asked to meet one-on-one to talk more about the faith. If the apologist had lost control of his anger, he likely would have lost the opportunity to speak with this young man and would have negatively impacted the rest of the audience. Here is a wonderful example of handling conflict—not with anger—but with love, humility, and by the power of the Spirit.

A hot-tempered man stirs up strife, but he who is slow to anger quiets contention.
Proverbs 15:18

Key Principles to Remember

1. When facing conflict, immediately do an anger check.

2. Be slow to anger.

3. Be gentle and soft-spoken in the face of another person's anger.

5

Control the Tongue

Let no corrupting talk come out of your mouths, but only
such as is good for building up. . . . And do not grieve
the Holy Spirit of God.
Ephesians 4:29-30

Conflict ignites fiery passions within the human soul. It can make the head throb, the blood boil, and the adrenaline rush. What is worse, conflict can turn the mouth into a weapon of mass destruction. Our words can become the primary weapon with which we "bite and devour one another" and damage relationships in the family of God. So no matter what the conflict, words matter—and they matter a lot.

I am convinced that most conflicts could be resolved with minimal damage to individual people and to the church if we brought both our anger and our tongue[1] under the Holy Spirit's control. In fact, *handling conflict biblically requires that we control our anger and our tongue.* The unholy war of words that is part of many disputes between God's people stands in opposition to the clear teaching of Scripture:

> Let no corrupting talk come out of your mouths, but only
> such as is good for building up, as fits the occasion, that it
> may give grace to those who hear. And do not grieve the
> Holy Spirit of God, by whom you were sealed for the day of
> redemption. (Eph. 4:29-30)

The Holy Spirit is sensitive to anything that damages or divides the people of God whom he has unified in Christ as one body and "sealed for the day of redemption."[2] Therefore, the Spirit cares deeply about how we speak to one another in the body of Christ. The possibility of grieving the Holy Spirit of God by what we say ought to be strong motivation for us to carefully choose our words and how we speak them.

---

[1] The *tongue* is a metaphor for speech.
[2] Eph. 2:16, 18; 4:30.

Our success in controlling our anger and speech is a clear measure of our desire to walk by the Spirit and to manage conflict in a Christlike manner (Gal. 5:16).

1. BRIDLE THE TONGUE

I was in a church history class where the teacher stated that Constantine, the first emperor of Rome to profess and then legalize Christianity, was not a true, born-again believer. Constantine, the teacher said, used Christianity for political advantage (ca. AD 285-337). One student disagreed with the teacher, insisting that Constantine was a true believer and a great leader in the history of Christianity. He became visibly upset and proceeded to attack the teacher verbally. The teacher, in turn, became angry and defensive. The exchange that ensued became so ugly and heated that the class was dismissed; teacher and student had to walk away from each other.

> Most conflicts could be resolved with minimal damage to individual people and to the church if we brought both our anger and our tongue under the Holy Spirit's control.

A week later, the teacher resumed the subject, stating that Constantine merely professed Christianity.

"Oh," the student exclaimed, "I thought you were talking about *Augustine*,[3] not Constantine. I thought you said *Augustine* was not a true believer."

"No," the teacher said, "I was talking about Constantine, not Augustine."

"Well then," the student said, "I agree with you."

The whole conflict occurred because each misunderstood the other! Neither one listened attentively and respectfully. Neither one seemed to care about the impact of his words or controlling his tongue.

Those of us who profess to be followers of Jesus Christ must remember that Jesus solemnly warns us that what we say reveals the attitude

---

[3]Augustine was Bishop of Hippo in North Africa (A.D. 354-430), and a genuine believer.

of our heart and that we will be held accountable for our every word:

> Out of the abundance of the heart the mouth speaks. . . . I tell you, on the day of judgment people will give account for every careless word they speak. (Matt. 12:34, 36)

The letter of James provides some of the most profound statements in all of Scripture regarding the control of the tongue. James describes the unrestrained tongue as "a fire, a world of unrighteousness . . . set on fire by hell . . . a restless evil, full of deadly poison" (James 3:6, 8). Out of such a mouth can spew gossip, rumors, lies, slander, cursing, and false accusations.

True spiritual godliness, in contrast, is demonstrated by bringing the tongue under control:

> If anyone thinks he is religious and does not bridle his tongue but deceives his heart, this person's religion is worthless. (James 1:26)

If we take pride in being "religious" but fail to control our tongue, we are deceiving ourselves. "Few things," writes John Blanchard, "give a clearer indication of the state of a man's heart than the words he speaks and the way in which he speaks them."[4]

Too often, when conflict erupts, people become angry and seem not to care what they say. At the very moment they need to bridle their tongue, they lose control and use words as weapons to hurt people. In such cases, James would bluntly say, "this person's religion is worthless." So whether a disagreement is serious or relatively insignificant, we must control our tongues. The person who controls the tongue is the truly spiritual believer, able to handle people and conflict constructively.

a. Be Quick to Hear

It's amazing how little we listen and how much we overreact to those who disagree with us. We immediately jump to justifying our position, defending our ego, and winning the argument. Even while the other

---

[4] John Blanchard, *Truth for Life: A Devotional Commentary on the Epistle of James* (Hertfordshire, UK: Evangelical Press, 1986), 103.

person is talking, we are not listening but are thinking about how we will answer. How foolish! "If one gives an answer before he hears, it is his folly and shame" (Prov. 18:13).

If the teacher in our story, for example, had asked the student some questions and given him a chance to explain his objections, their disagreement could have been settled quickly. The student also could have asked the teacher to explain his position more fully. Instead, neither person showed much interest in listening to the other. Each one needed to exercise control of his tongue by being, in the words of James, "quick to hear" and "slow to speak" (James 1:19).

In his great wisdom, King Solomon observes: "The purpose in a man's heart is like deep water, but a man of understanding will draw it out" (Prov. 20:5). So a "man of understanding"—a wise person—doesn't need to do all the talking. A wise person listens well and doesn't interrupt. A truly wise person asks the right questions in order to understand what the other person is saying and see the situation from the other person's point of view.

> "If one gives an answer before he hears, it is his folly and shame."
> Proverbs 18:13

A wise person also considers the possibility that the other person may be right! Not one of us thinks straight all of the time. When we are open to learning, our opponent may turn out to be our best teacher. So those who are wise seek to honestly understand the other person's arguments, reasoning, and position.

b. Be Slow to Speak

Not only are we to be "quick to hear," we also are to be "slow to speak." This means that most of us will need to make a determined effort not to be like the teacher and student who were quick to speak, accuse, and insult. We will need to learn to be slow to spout our opinions, slow to be the first to answer, slow to dominate a conversation, and slow to pronounce judgment.

Although we may love to hear ourselves talk, Solomon warns of the dangers of too much talk:

• When words are many, transgression is not lacking, but whoever

restrains his lips is prudent. (Prov. 10:19)
- Whoever keeps his mouth and his tongue keeps himself out of trouble. (Prov. 21:23)

- Whoever restrains his words has knowledge. (Prov. 17:27)

- Whoever guards his mouth preserves his life. (Prov. 13:3)

- A fool's lips walk into a fight, and his mouth invites a beating. (Prov. 18:6)

Wise people benefit when they control their tongue. Fools, however, lack restraint, which leads to conflict.

Controlling the tongue is difficult, even impossible, for those without the Holy Spirit. James writes, "No human being can tame the tongue," and goes on to describe it as "a restless evil, full of deadly poison" (James 3:8). James is not exaggerating. An uncontrolled tongue destroys families and friendships and can wreak havoc on a church body. If, however, we have the Holy Spirit indwelling us, we have God's power to help us control the untamable tongue. May our prayer be that of the psalmist:

> Set a guard, O Lord, over my mouth; keep watch over the door of my lips! (Ps. 141:3)

2. CHOOSE THE RIGHT WORDS

Speech is a marvelous gift. It distinguishes us from the animal world and provides evidence that we bear the divine image of God. It also gives evidence of a believer's new life in Christ. God intends the believer's "new self" to be displayed in the way we speak,[5] especially when we are engaged in emotionally stirring conflict with our brothers and sisters in Christ.

When conflict arises, the way we speak determines whether a potentially explosive situation is moderated or escalates. To answer

---

[5]Eph. 4:29; 5:4; 1 Tim. 4:12; Titus 2:7-8; James 3:9-10.

angry words with more angry words only throws wood on the fire of contention. "A harsh word stirs up anger" (Prov. 15:1). *So we are not to respond to mean, nasty talk with more mean, nasty talk; we are not to return evil words for evil words.*[6] Instead, we are to overcome evil with good. Our speech is to be wholesome and healing—building up others, not tearing them down. When we are verbally attacked, we bless; when persecuted, we endure; when slandered, we respond with kindness and self-control (1 Cor. 4:12-13).

Handling conflict biblically requires that we know and respond appropriately to the power of words: "Death and life are in the power of the tongue" (Prov. 18:21). Cutting words create conflict; harsh, inflammatory words exacerbate it; gossip poisons relationships and drives people apart. Kind and gracious words have a calming effect—persuading, assuaging, and ultimately bringing peace and reconciliation.

a. Eliminate Cutting Words from Your Vocabulary

The tongue is one of the cruelest weapons humans possess, and "the wounds that sharp words inflict are among the most painful experiences of men."[7] Cruel, cutting words can remain in a person's mind and spoil relationships forever. Although some people take pride in their ability to shred others with their razor-sharp wit and cutting comments, Proverbs 12:18 warns against people "whose rash words are like sword thrusts [intended to wound and kill]."

> **When conflict arises, the way we speak determines whether a potentially explosive situation is moderated or escalates.**

After years of experience in facing painful controversy, Francis Schaeffer makes this insightful comment regarding the power of cutting words:

> I have observed one thing *among true Christians* in their differences in many countries: what divides and severs true Christian groups and Christians—what leaves a bitterness

---

[6]Luke 6:28-29; Matt. 5:38-42; 1 Cor. 4:12; Rom. 12:17, 21; 1 Thess. 5:15; 1 Peter 3:9.
[7]H. C. Leupold, *Exposition of the Psalms* (Grand Rapids: Baker, 1969), 262.

that can last for twenty, thirty, or forty years. . . . Invariably it is lack of love—and the bitter things that are said by true Christians in the midst of differences. These stick in the mind like glue.[8]

The Holy Spirit does not lead believers to make cruel, mean, nasty, or insulting comments. Such talk is "the work of the flesh," not the Spirit. The Holy Spirit desires that a Christian be "a model of . . . sound speech" (Titus 2:7-8). This means that we do not refer to fellow believers with whom we disagree with such rude epithets as "losers," "idiots," "heretics," or "liberals." God's people are to love one another, and love "is not arrogant or rude" (1 Cor. 13:4-5). James conveys the Holy Spirit's mind over such misuse of the tongue when he writes,

> With it we bless our Lord and Father, and with it we curse people who are made in the likeness of God. From the same mouth come blessing and cursing. My brothers, these things ought not to be so. (James 3:9-10)

To gain victory over a cutting tongue, eliminate from your daily vocabulary all unnecessary terms of disparagement—all words that belittle, mock, insult, or demean God's people. The "battle for vocal holiness," states Sinclair Ferguson, "is a long-running one, and it needs to be waged incessantly, daily, hourly."[9] Should you catch yourself using any derogatory words, do not rationalize such unholy talk but confess it as sin that grieves the Spirit of God. Remember, the mouth simply expresses what is in the heart (Luke 6:45), and sin is at the root of wrong speaking.

b. Beware of Inflammatory Speech

Anyone who is serious about handling conflict in a Christ-honoring

---

[8]Francis A. Schaeffer, *The Mark of the Christian*, in *The Complete Works*, Vol. 4, Book 3 (Westchester, IL: Crossway, 1983), 195.

[9]Sinclair B. Ferguson, "The Bit, the Bridle, and the Blessing: An Exposition of James 3:1-12," in *The Power of Words and the Wonder of God*, ed. John Piper and Justin Taylor (Wheaton, IL: Crossway, 2009), 48.

way must beware of exaggerated or inflammatory speech because it provokes anger and distracts from the true issues at hand. Consider the following examples of how important it is to speak accurately rather than in exaggerated terms.

Members of a particular church were caught up in a fight over music styles. They simultaneously complained that the music was too fast, too slow, too old, too new, too loud, or too soft! One prominent older woman accused the song leader of playing "rock and roll," prompting someone else to say that the church had become "like a nightclub." Meanwhile, a young man complained that the music director chose "funeral dirges" that turned people off to worship. None of these exaggerated, inflammatory claims were true. None were helpful to church leaders who sought to end the music war. All such preposterous rhetoric is polarizing and frustrating to people who are trying to work toward resolution.

Speaking truthfully, without exaggeration, is most important when addressing doctrinal differences. Adherents on both sides of the debate over the doctrine of divine election and human free will, for example, often resort to extreme, inflammatory language. Some of the Arminian persuasion, who emphasize free will, state that Calvinists base their beliefs on the Greek philosophy of determinism and ignore the Scriptures. This infuriates the Calvinists who emphasize God's sovereignty in election. Some Calvinists, in turn, call Arminians heretics and presume to say they don't think Arminians are born-again believers because of their works-oriented salvation. This infuriates the Arminians. All such language is misguided and toxic. It is never helpful for discussing profitably the truths of Scripture among those who love God and his Word.

> Beware of exaggerated or inflammatory speech that provokes anger and distracts from the true issues at hand.

All believers are responsible before God to use accurate, temperate language in our disagreements with one another. Exaggerated, inflammatory speech may play well in secular politics and may serve the purposes of paranoid religious fanatics who lie and kill, but such language is not acceptable for those who profess "the word of the truth, the gospel" (Col.1:5) and are created in "the likeness of God and true righteousness and holiness" (Eph. 4:24).

God hates all forms of lying speech: "The LORD detests lying lips, but he delights in men who are truthful" (Prov. 12:22 NIV). Our gospel is the gospel of truth, and our God is the God of truth, so he requires us to speak the truth to one another in love (Eph. 4:15). Exaggerated speech is a form of falsehood that distorts truth. There can be nothing righteous or holy about it. Inflammatory words are "fighting words" that fuel conflict and further polarize people. They don't solve problems, they only make them worse. So it is imperative that believers refuse to engage in exaggerated and inflammatory speech.

If you want to gain victory over this type of sin, eliminate inflammatory statements about other people's beliefs. Do not misrepresent or distort them. In daily conversation, practice speaking accurately and truthfully—the way the Holy Spirit always leads us to do.

c. Don't Gossip

D. E. Hoste, the successor to Hudson Taylor who founded the China Inland Mission, was a student of human behavior. An extraordinarily skilled people manager, Hoste was responsible for more than a thousand missionaries across China. Reflecting on one of the most troubling problems the mission had faced in China, he wrote:

> Looking back over these fifty years, I really think that if I were asked to mention one thing which has done more harm and occasioned more sorrow and division in God's work than anything else, I should say tale-bearing.[10]

Gossip, or talebearing, is one of the common sins of discord. It is a work of the flesh (2 Cor. 12:20). Like a dreadful, contagious disease, it poisons people's minds and creates chaos and misinformation. It is an ugly vice that drives people apart and destroys peace. Proverbs condemns it as a malicious act that "separates close friends" (Prov. 16:28; 17:9). It can do great damage to the believing community, particularly when

---

[10]Phyllis Thompson, *D. E. Hoste, 'A Prince with God'* (London: China Inland Mission, 1947), 121.

conflict arises.

It is disheartening to hear the misinformation, half-truths, innuendos, exaggerations, distorted facts, and outright lies that circulate among God's people, especially today on the Internet. The tongue truly is "a fire . . . a restless evil, full of deadly poison" (James 3:6, 8). Once started, the fire is difficult to extinguish—even with the truth.

One of the fastest ways to stop gossip and the division it creates is to not repeat it: "For lack of wood the fire goes out, and where there is no whisperer, quarreling ceases" (Prov. 26:20). But most of us have a perverse enjoyment of gossip, and Scripture warns that it is as hard to resist as the most appealing pastries: "The words of a whisperer are like delicious morsels" (Prov. 26:22). A leader in a church characterized by years of destructive infighting readily attests to this. "We have a church full of people," he told me, "who feed like vultures on gossip." Until people face their sinful appetite for gossip and repent, quarreling will not cease.

In order to gain victory over gossip, we must not participate in it. We must eliminate gossip from our daily conversations, and we must steer clear of those who are talebearers. Proverbs warns us to "not associate with a simple babbler" (Prov. 20:19), whom Bruce Waltke terms a "silly chatterer."[11]

d. Use Gracious, Edifying Words

In our media-saturated world where arrogant talking heads shout people down, reduce complex issues to one-liners, and demonize their opponents to cheering crowds, there are precious few role models of gracious and truthful speech. So Paul's encouragement to Timothy to "set the believers an example in speech" (1 Tim. 4:12) ought also to encourage us to be an example of speaking with gracious, true, and edifying words. Wholesome words have the power to calm tempers, heal wounds, resolve conflicts, persuade opponents, and bring people together. They exert great power when they are used for "building up" members of the body of Christ and giving "grace to those who hear"

---

[11]Bruce K. Waltke, *The Book of Proverbs Chapter 1-15*, NICOT (Grand Rapids: Eerdmans, 2004), 1: 148.

(Eph. 4:29).

Consider the implications of the following insight on gracious, edifying words when it comes to resolving conflict:

- Gentle, conciliatory words can calm an angry person: "A soft answer turns away wrath" (Prov. 15:1).

- Gracious words can comfort a sick and wounded heart: "The tongue of the wise brings healing" (Prov. 12:18), and "Anxiety in a man's heart weighs him down, but a good word makes him glad" (Prov. 12:25). Gracious words "are like a honeycomb, sweetness to the soul and health to the body" (Prov. 16:24).

- Pleasant words increase persuasiveness (Prov. 16:21). Gentle, patient words can break down the hardest arguments and win over the most resistant opponent: "With patience a ruler may be persuaded, and a soft tongue will break a bone" (Prov. 25:15).

So if you want to win and persuade people in a godly manner, speak with gracious, edifying, encouraging words. Choose your words wisely and consider how to build up others, not tear them down. Learn to speak as a peacemaker, encourager, admonisher, and comforter. Graciously bless even those who speak evil against you.

When facing conflict, determine beforehand to always speak the truth. *Truthfulness is the foundation of all edifying speech.* "Truthful speech" is the characteristic of all true "servants of God" and God-honoring "ministry" (2 Cor. 6:3-4, 7). Conflict can be managed in a Christ-honoring way if we choose to use wholesome words of truth and grace.

3. SPEAKING STERNLY IN LOVE

It might seem contradictory that Paul spoke repeatedly of forbearance,

---

[12]1 Cor. 3:1-4; 4:8, 10, 18-21; 5; 6:1-8; 15:34; 2 Cor. 11:4, 19-20; 12:20-21; 13:1-3.

gentleness, and love, yet when he wrote to the Corinthians (and to the Galatians) he used stern, even sarcastic, language.[12] To understand this seeming discrepancy, we must realize that during Paul's absence the Corinthians drifted into the dangerous waters of worldly wisdom. They began to deny, in attitude and in practice, the implications of the gospel (1 Cor. 1-4). They also came under the influence of false apostles, agents of Satan, who criticized Paul's authority and gospel.[13]

To awaken the proud Corinthians from the deadly influence of false apostles and their own stubborn waywardness, Paul used pointed language to startle them out of their self-deception. They were on the verge of self-destruction. He wrote sternly in order to awaken them to reality. So his letters to his wayward converts were not harsh, arrogant rants. They were masterful examples of tact and skill in firm, tough, loving persuasion.

a. Paul Wrote Sternly but in Love

Paul wrote sternly and sarcastically out of his deep love and concern for his "beloved children" in the gospel (1 Cor. 4:14). He loved them more than his own life. He wrote this way on limited occasions because of his special relationship with them as their spiritual father.[14] Roy Zuck notes, "These stern rebukes or severe warnings . . . were not inconsistent with his love. They stemmed from his love."[15]

Although Paul was compelled to rebuke and speak sternly to the Corinthians, he could not stop himself from alternately pouring out his loving heart with the most tender, endearing statements. For example:

- I do not say this to condemn you, for I said before that you are in our hearts, to die together and to live together. (2 Cor. 7:3)

- I seek not what is yours but you. . . . I will most gladly spend and be spent for your souls. If I love you more, am I to be loved less? (2 Cor. 12:14-15)[16]

---

[13]2 Cor. 10:2, 10; 11:12-15; 12:11, 17-19; 13:3.
[14]1 Cor. 4:14-16; 9:1-3; 2 Cor. 3:1-3; 10:14; 11:2.
[15]Roy Zuck, *Teaching as Paul Taught* (Grand Rapids: Baker, 1998), 104.
[16]See also 2 Cor. 2:4; 6:11; 11:11.

Although the Corinthians may have been tempted to think that Paul despised them, he reassured them of his tender love by stating it in the most personal and affectionate terms. Thus Paul ends the letter of 1 Corinthians by saying, "My love be with you all in Christ Jesus. Amen" (1 Cor. 16:24).

b. Paul Wrote Sternly with Tears

It pained Paul greatly to use severe language in his letters to his beloved spiritual children (2 Cor. 12:11). The extraordinary letter of 2 Corinthians gives us unusual insight into the depth of Paul's love. He writes:

> For I wrote to you out of much affliction and anguish of heart and with many tears, not to cause you pain but to let you know the abundant love that I have for you. (2 Cor. 2:4; also 7:8)

And to his beloved Galatians he confesses, "My little children, for whom I am again in the anguish of childbirth until Christ is formed in you! I wish I could . . . change my tone" (Gal. 4:19-20).

Paul was not a passive leader who would not stand up to troublesome people or false teachers of the gospel. Although he would rather come to his wayward converts with "love in a spirit of gentleness," he was fully prepared to use a "rod" of discipline.[17] However, he preferred not to use his apostolic authority to discipline with severity:

> Conflict can be managed in a Christ-honoring way if we choose to use wholesome words of truth and grace.

> For this reason I write these things while I am away from you, that when I come I may not have to be severe in my use of the authority that the Lord has given me for building up and not for tearing down. (2 Cor. 13:10)

---

[17] 1 Cor. 4:21. See also 2 Cor. 1:23-24; 2:1-4, 10; 4:5, 12, 15; 5:13; 6:3-13; 7:3; 10:1, 8; 11:7-9; 12:14-15, 17-19; 13:7, 9-10.

Paul didn't enjoy being severe or sarcastic, and he had no interest in showing off his knowledge. He wrote to the Corinthians out of "much anguish of heart and with many tears" (2 Cor. 2:4). He mourned over their sin and prayed for their "restoration" (2 Cor. 13:9). All that he said and did was for their edification.[18]

When Paul's letters succeeded in leading the Corinthians to repent and amend their ways (2 Cor. 7:8-13), he was overjoyed. So it should be with us. Love and concern must be our motive whenever we must rebuke or speak pointedly to fellow believers about their stubborn waywardness or erroneous beliefs. Even when we must speak sternly, we must control our tongue and choose our words carefully to ensure that all we do is "done in love" (1 Cor. 16:14).

Set the believers an example in speech.
1 Timothy 4:12

Key Principles to Remember

1. When facing conflict, be quick to hear and slow to speak.

2. Guard your tongue against using cutting words or inflammatory language.

3. Speak graciously and truthfully using words that edify, heal, and unite.

---

[18]2 Cor. 1:23-24; 2:1-2, 10; 7:8-12; 10:8.

6

Control the Criticism

Do not speak evil against one another.
James 4:11

While visiting a friend's farm, I noticed that some of the chickens running around were missing feathers. Some even had open sores on their skin. When I asked the reason for this, the farmer casually replied, "Oh, they like to peck at one another." That's exactly the way some people treat one another: They like to peck at others! They love to find fault, criticize, complain, and condemn. In fact, anyone who has served in a church has encountered petty complainers and faultfinding critics who act more like pecking chickens than Spirit-filled believers.

Faultfinding critics have an amazing ability to gather a flock of contentious complainers, and they can wield fearsome destructive power in a church. They seem to think that they are doing God and the angels a great service by pointing out and criticizing others' faults. Scripture, however, says otherwise. James admonishes us not to "speak evil against," or "grumble against one another" (James 4:11; 5:9). Paul warns us not to "pass judgment on one another any longer" (Rom. 14:13). Titus 3:2 instructs us "to speak evil of no one"—believer or nonbeliever. God doesn't want his Spirit-indwelt children to be known as people who slander, criticize, and bad-mouth others.

If we desire to display Christlike character, *we must not only control our anger and tongue when we face conflict, we also have to control a critical, judgmental, or complaining spirit.* Not all criticism or judging is wrong; at times rebuke or constructive criticism is necessary and right. But slanderous criticism, hypocritical judgments, and self-centered complaining are extremely divisive and sinful vices. They are a particularly malicious way by which we bite and devour one another.

1. STOP SPEAKING EVIL OF OTHERS

God requires that his holy people love and care for one another, not hate and slander each other. The Mosaic laws for practical, holy living prohibit slander and hate:

> You shall be holy, for I the Lord your God am holy. . . .
> You shall not go around as a slanderer among your people.
> And you shall not stand up against the life of your neighbor: I am the Lord.
> You shall not hate your brother in your heart, but you shall reason frankly with your neighbor, lest you incur sin because of him. You shall not take vengeance or bear a grudge against the sons of your own people, but you shall love your neighbor as yourself: I am the Lord. (Lev. 19:2, 16-18; also Ps. 101:5; Prov. 10:18)

Moses knew from bitter personal experience how badly the Israelites needed to heed these instructions. No matter what he did, the Israelites found fault with him. Many times they slandered his motives and mercilessly criticized his leadership ability. Through slander and unjust criticism they pecked away at him until he wanted to die (Num. 11:10-15).

> God doesn't want his Spirit-indwelt children to be known as people who slander, criticize, and bad-mouth others.

God's commands against slander and hate were necessary because the Israelites would become a cohesive, holy society only if they loved and honored one another.[1] Hate and slander would corrupt God's holy nation. In the New Testament, James takes his cue from Leviticus 19 and with equal clarity forbids slander among God's people:

> Do not speak evil against one another, brothers. The one who speaks against a brother or judges his brother, speaks evil against the law and judges the law. But if you judge the law,

---

[1] See also Est. 3:8-9; Ps. 50:19-20; 55:21; 59:7; 64:3-4; 140:3, 11; Prov. 10:18; 20:19; Jer. 9:3-6, 8; 18:18.

you are not a doer of the law but a judge. There is only one lawgiver and judge, he who is able to save and to destroy. But who are you to judge your neighbor? (James 4:11-12)

James forbids any kind of slanderous or degrading talk including derogatory remarks, false criticism, defamation of character, putting people down, or false accusations.[2]

Most Christians don't realize how much slander hurts people and stirs up malicious contention. It truly is a devilish force for community destruction.[3] John Blanchard, a well-traveled evangelist, remarks that, "There is a shameful amount of slander that goes on within our Christian organizations today and the result is always marred relationship."[4]

Despite these warnings, some believers are in such a habit of criticizing and speaking badly of others that they think it is normal behavior. But it is not! All such speech is a work of the flesh (2 Cor. 12:20). Slander is the devil's work (even the word devil means "accuser" or "slanderer"). The devil is the relentless accuser of God's people, and he incessantly "accuses them day and night before our God" (Rev. 12:10).

The Holy Spirit does not lead believers to speak evil of others, or to be self-righteous faultfinders or harsh critics. Scripture teaches that believers are to "outdo one another in showing honor" (Rom. 12:10). By choosing to show honor rather than to slander or criticize, we promote love and harmony among brothers and sisters. Allow me to share an example of this principle at work.

Our church was started by a group of families who left their former church due to frustration with many unaddressed issues and serious problems. None of these families intended to start a new church,

---

[2]"Speak evil against," from the verb *katalaleō*: "speak ill of, speak degradingly of, speak evil of, defame, slander" (BDAG, 519). The noun form, *katalalia*, is found in 2 Corinthians 12:20 and 1 Peter 2:1 and is translated as "slander."
[3]According to 1 Corinthians 5:11, an unrepentant "reviler" or slanderer is to be disciplined by the church: "Reviler," from the Greek word *loidoros*: "reviler, abusive person" (BDAG, 602). A reviler speaks abusively and maliciously of another person in order to hurt, tear down, or destroy. Reviling is sin. Some English translations render this word "slanderer."
[4]John Blanchard, *Truth For Life* (Hertfordshire, UK: Evangelical Press, 1986), 305.

but a year later they started to meet regularly for Bible study. From that seed, a new congregation grew.

Early on, the leaders made a covenant between themselves not to criticize their former church, not to speak evil of any of its members, and not to carry on any form of verbal warfare. They knew that criticism would damage many family relationships (some members of the fledgling church had family members who still attended their former church) and destroy any hope for future unity. As a result, our church started on a positive note. Within seven years, the two churches were in pleasant fellowship and able to work together for the gospel.

This is a good example of how unity can be maintained, or restored, when Christians refuse to slander or unnecessarily criticize. I find it remarkable that I joined the church after it had been meeting for six years and heard nothing about the division from the previous church until nearly two years after that! This model of Christian conduct and speech by the church's first leaders laid the proper foundational attitudes and behaviors for the next generation to follow, which they did.

2. STOP JUDGING ONE ANOTHER

"Slander and judgmentalism are close cousins," writes Dan McCartney.[5] Hence James prohibits both speaking evil of another and unlawfully judging others:

> Do not speak evil against one another, brothers. The one who speaks against a brother or judges his brother, speaks evil against the law and judges the law. But if you judge the law, you are not a doer of the law but a judge. . . . But who are you to judge your neighbor? (James 4:11-12)

To "judge" in this sense is to unnecessarily or inappropriately condemn a brother or sister by judging the person's motives or appearances, or to judge with the wrong attitude or for the wrong reason. It is making judgmental statements about another that are not rightfully ours to make. Such unlawful judging is the cause of much relational conflict and

[5]Dan G. McCartney, *James*, BECNT (Grand Rapids: Baker, 2009), 220.

congregational infighting. As James knew very well, harsh, judgmental attitudes were a characteristic sin of the Pharisees. He didn't want to see this self-righteous, condemnatory attitude spread among the early believing communities to which he wrote.

a. Don't Judge Like the Pharisees

The Pharisees were the ultimate critics and faultfinders. They loved to judge nearly everyone. Their judgments were quick, harsh, negative, and unmerciful. They were experts at condemning others for minor infractions of the law while they themselves, Jesus said, violated "the weightier matters of the law" (Matt. 23:23). Thus they were hypocritical judges who quickly found fault with others while they minimized or ignored their own sins.

In one of the best-known passages in the Sermon on the Mount, our Lord warned his disciples against having the judgmental spirit of the Pharisees that is so destructive to the family of God:

> Judge not, that you be not judged. . . . Why do you see the speck that is in your brother's eye, but do not notice the log that is in your own eye? . . . You hypocrite, first take the log out of your own eye, and then you will see clearly to take the speck out of your brother's eye. (Matt. 7:1, 3, 5)

Jesus forbids despising and condemning others for their shortcomings while failing to see one's own glaring sins. *He does not want his disciples to be like the hypocritical Pharisees who were harsh, critical, unmerciful, and self-righteous and yet were spiritually blind to their own sinful condition.* However, what Jesus teaches in Matthew 7 regarding judgmentalism is commonly misunderstood. The pervasive attitude of "non-judgmentalism" in Western society leads us to believe that any judgment regarding doctrine is frowned upon. We must not forget that the gospel would be lost to the world and the church would be assimilated into secular society if we did not make proper judgments regarding good and evil, moral conduct, and doctrine.

Distinguishing between proper and improper judging can be confusing, but to illustrate the differences we only need to look at 1

Corinthians 4 and 5 for instruction. In response to the Corinthians' incorrect judgment of his ministry and success in the gospel, Paul says, "do not pronounce judgment before the time, before the Lord comes, who will bring to light the things now hidden in darkness and will disclose the purposes of the heart" (1 Cor. 4:5). The Corinthians did not have sufficient knowledge or facts to judge Paul's motives or success, so in this situation they were judging where they had no right to judge. In a different situation, where judging was clearly called for, Paul rebuked the Corinthians for failing to censure one of their members who was participating in immoral sexual behavior (1 Cor. 5:3, 12-13).

Like Jesus and Paul, James does not forbid "right judgment." He sternly denounces sinful behavior and calls his readers to repent. At the same time, he forbids slander, abusive speech, and judgmental statements that are not rightfully ours to make against a brother or sister in Christ.

b. Don't Judge One Another over Disputable Matters

While home on furlough, a missionary found himself caught in the middle of a debate regarding Christian liberty. One group insisted that their church not celebrate Christmas because it was originally a pagan holiday and had become increasingly secularized. Another group claimed liberty to celebrate the holiday because it no longer had pagan connotations. The missionary was forced to take sides, and when he did, the opposing group declared him to be a traitor and false teacher who was no longer welcome at the

> "God . . . grant you to live in such harmony with one another . . . that together you may with one voice glorify the God and Father of our Lord Jesus Christ."
> Romans 15:5-7

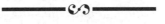

church. One angry person even launched a website that listed all of the missionary's alleged sins, failures, and erroneous beliefs and advised people not to support the missionary.

This missionary's experience is nothing new. Among Jewish and Gentile Christians in first-century Rome, controversy raged over the observance of dietary laws, drinking wine, and the celebration of holy days (Rom. 14:1-15:13). The Jewish Christians displayed a harsh, judgmental attitude toward the eating habits and certain lifestyle choices of their Gentile brothers and sisters who had been converted out of paganism. Paul describes these Jewish believers as "weak in faith" (Rom. 14:1).[6] The Gentile Christians acted no better, showing contempt for the traditional dietary laws and holy days of their Jewish brothers and sisters. As the majority group, the Gentiles put considerable pressure on the minority group to conform to their way of thinking. Paul calls them the "strong" (Rom. 15:1) because of their understanding of the practical implications of the gospel of grace, new life in the Spirit, and freedom in Christ. Even though Paul agreed with the "strong" about the theological issue of clean versus unclean foods,[7] *he totally opposed their loveless behavior and contempt for those with whom they differed.*

Christians still argue and separate over topics of debate that Paul refers to as "opinions" (or "disputed matters," NIV).[8] These are not fundamental doctrines or issues of moral failure such as lying, stealing, or sexual immorality. Rather, these are secondary issues of personal conscience and conviction such as Sabbath keeping, celebrating Christmas, drinking alcohol, dancing, lifting hands in worship, hanging pictures of Jesus on the wall, honoring ancestors, schooling children, proper dress and hair styles, forms of entertainment, recreational choices, or even the use of leavened or unleavened communion bread. Just as in the first-century, Christians today often exhibit arrogant, harsh, judgmental attitudes toward those with whom we disagree regarding these issues.

It is all too easy to fight and divide over peripheral matters of lifestyle and traditional religious practices. It is disgraceful that some Christians cannot praise God with their fellow brothers and sisters in worship because of disagreements over such "disputed matters." We must remember that "the kingdom of God is not a matter of eating and drinking but of righteousness and peace and joy in the Holy Spirit. . . .

---

[6] By "weak in faith," he means that they have a deficient understanding of the practical implications of the gospel of the grace of God, especially as it deals with their over-scrupulous Jewish traditions of kosher foods and observance of certain holy days.

[7] Rom. 14:14, 20; 1 Cor. 8:8.

[8] It is difficult to know precisely how to translate the last two words in Romans 14:1 of the Greek text (*diakriseis dialogismōn*). The ESV rendering is "not to quarrel over opinions." The NIV translates the words as "without passing judgment on disputable matters." The NIV is to be preferred.

So then let us pursue what makes for peace and for mutual upbuilding"
(Rom. 14:17-19).

One purpose of Paul's letter to the Romans was to foster unity
among Jewish and Gentile believers despite their lifestyle differences:

> May the God of endurance and encouragement grant you to
> live in such harmony with one another, in accord with Christ
> Jesus, that together you may with one voice glorify the God
> and Father of our Lord Jesus Christ. Therefore welcome one
> another as Christ has welcomed you, for the glory of God.
> (Rom. 15:5-7)

*What a testimony to the truth and power of the gospel that tradition-
minded Jewish Christians and formerly pagan Gentile Christians could
accept one another and together worship God "with one voice"!* For these
Jewish and Gentile Christians to have broken into separate factions,
each condemning the other over secondary issues, would have been a
violation of the gospel message of reconciliation. If God expected Jewish
and Gentile believers, despite their historical and cultural divergence,
to accept one another and glorify God together in worship, how much
more does he expect believers today, traditionalist and progressive, to put
aside our petty differences and do the same. Thus, we are free to disagree
over "disputable matters," but we are not free to use inflammatory
speech, to speak evil of one another, or to divide God's family.

3. STOP GRUMBLING AND QUARRELING

The World Trade Center in New York City took six long years to build, but
it was destroyed in only 90 minutes on September 11, 2001. In a similar
way, a local church that has taken a lifetime to build can be devastated in a
few months by a sinful firestorm of complaining and quarreling.

Grumbling (or complaining) is not constructive or edifying to the
family of God. Like a contagious disease, grumbling generates conflict,
confusion, and unhappiness that quickly spread throughout a church
body until all are infected with discontent. J. A. Motyer points out that,
"Nowhere does the self-centered heart of man more quickly take control

than through the machinery of criticism."[9] Grumbling, Motyer goes on to say, is associated with "selfish complaining, unbalanced criticism of small matters, impatience towards what is not understood, grudging unwillingness to be helpful."[10]

In recognition of the damaging effects grumbling has upon a Christian congregation, James writes: "Do not grumble against one another, brothers, so that you may not be judged; behold, the Judge is standing at the door" (James 5:9). Like James, Paul also forbids grumbling and arguing. He admonishes believers to "Do all things without grumbling or questioning" (Phil. 2:14).

Problems in the church at Philippi led to disgruntled complaining against each other and most likely against the church leaders. So Paul warns the Philippian church not to act like the Israelites who grumbled about the weather, the food, the water, the desert, the heat, and their leaders.[11] Their complaining was not constructive, nor was it done properly. Rather, it expressed their collective unbelief, lack of gratitude, and continual rebellion against those whom God had placed in authority over them.

In addition to grumbling, Paul also addresses "questioning," which is better rendered in Philippians 2:14 as "arguing" or "quarreling."[12] Grumbling often leads to petty, childish arguments and quarrels. Apparently the Philippians got caught up in a cycle of petty complaints and quarreling and needed Paul's admonition to stop.

Just as grumbling and quarreling nearly destroyed Moses and the nation of Israel, and threatened the church at Philippi, *these two vices destroy many church leaders and congregations today*. Often, one of the reasons pastors and other workers leave Christian ministry is that they can no longer bear the petty complaints and constant arguing among

---

[9]J. A. Motyer, *The Message of Philippians: Jesus our Joy*, BST (Downers Grove, IL: IVP, 1984), 131.

[10]Ibid., 132.

[11]The noun "grumbling," *gongysmos*, is plural, "grumblings." It is used here of "complaint, displeasure, expressed in murmuring" (BDAG, 204). See also Acts 6:1; 1 Peter 4:9. The verb form appears in 1 Corinthians 10:10, which is reminiscent of Numbers 14:1-38.

[12]"Questioning," *dialogismos*, can also be translated "dispute" or "argument" (BDAG, 232), or "quarrelling." It seems that this is what the context requires, although it is a rarer usage of this Greek term. The word is plural, "disputes," "quarrels." See also 1 Timothy 2:8 and Luke 9:46 for similar use.

the people. So if we want to guard ourselves and our churches from the selfish spirit of grumbling and quarreling, we must decide, in simple obedience to God's Word, to do "all things" without grumbling and quarreling.

At the end of Paul's letter to the Philippians, he highlights several ways to overcome sinful grumbling and quarreling. He advocates (1) rejoicing always and in all circumstances (Phil. 4:4), (2) displaying gentle forbearance (v. 5), (3) prayer, supplication, and thanksgiving (vv. 6-7), (4) godly contentment in all circumstances (vv. 11-12), and (5) thinking on all that is good and excellent (v. 8).

If rejoicing, prayer, forbearance, godly contentment in all circumstances, and deliberate reflection on all that is good and right characterized those of us who call ourselves Christians, how much healthier our churches would be! How much less conflict our churches would experience!

4. HOW TO REBUKE AND CRITICIZE CONSTRUCTIVELY

Although we are not to "speak evil against one another" or "judge" improperly, there are times when it is necessary and legitimate to admonish, rebuke, judge, or constructively criticize (to point out a fault). To refuse to do such is to fail those whom we love or are responsible to lead.[13] All forms of criticism or rebuke, however, need to be done in a biblically directed way that is helpful and not hurtful. Happily, the Bible provides basic guidelines for constructive and effective criticism.

a. Pray

All criticism and rebuke needs to be bathed in prayer. Be assured that God is quite willing to help you know how to speak and act in difficult situations when you look to him. James 1:5 says, "If any of you lacks wisdom, let him ask God, who gives generously to all without reproach, and it will be given him." So before you correct or judge, pray for wisdom, courage, and tact. Pray that the Lord would prepare the other

---

[13]*Admonish*: Acts 20:31; Col. 3:16. *Correct*: 2 Tim. 2:24-25; 3:16. *Rebuke*: Mark 8:33; Luke 9:55; 17:3; 2 Tim. 4:2; Titus 1:9, 13.

person to receive correction. In the words of Donald Carson, "All of us would be wiser if we would resolve never to put people down, except on our prayer lists."[14]

b. Check Your Attitudes and Motives

All criticism and rebuke needs to be done with the right attitude and for the right reasons. Criticism given with an attitude of pride, vindictiveness, or anger will hurt the other person and accomplish little. Criticism must be given with an attitude of humility that demonstrates the fruit of the Spirit and conveys Christian love.

Furthermore, criticism must be given for the other person's good. If you seek only to "punish" the other person, you are violating basic biblical rules of conduct. Paul wrote his severe letter of rebuke to the Corinthians "out of much affliction and anguish of heart and with many tears" to let them "know the abundant love" he had for them (2 Cor. 2:4). His criticism and rebuke arose from a deep, fatherly love for the Corinthians, not out of an emotional need to pay them back for all the pain they had caused him. Indeed, everything he did for the Corinthians was for their "upbuilding" (2 Cor. 12:19).

Before we offer any criticism, we should ask: Is it necessary that I comment critically about a certain person? Is it my place to criticize? Have I fallen into a sinful habit of faultfinding and criticizing others? Does my criticism of another brother or sister violate the commands of Scripture (Lev. 19:16)?

c. Speak Gently

All criticism and rebuke needs to be done with gentleness. Gentleness is a fruit of the Spirit (Gal. 5:23), and the New Testament emphasizes the importance of dealing with people and their problems with gentleness.[15] To be gentle is to be kind, tender, gracious, calm, and not harsh or combative. People do not respond well to harsh, arrogant critics, but

---

[14]D. A. Carson, *A Call to Spiritual Reformation: Priorities from Paul and His Prayers* (Grand Rapids: Baker, 1992), 29.
[15] 1 Cor. 4:21; 2 Cor. 10:1; Gal. 6:1; Eph. 4:2; 1 Thess. 2:7; 1 Tim. 3:3; 6:11; 2 Tim. 2:25; Titus 3:2; James 3:17; 1 Peter 3:4, 16.

gentle correction makes a person more receptive to consider a change of mind and heart.

d. Balance Criticism with Words of Encouragement

When criticism or rebuke is needed, give careful thought to the words you use. Make no mistake that "death and life are in the power of the tongue" (Prov. 18:21). Remember that "rash words are like sword thrusts, but the tongue of the wise brings healing" (Prov. 12:18). Harsh or exaggerated words turn people off to correction; choice words bring calm to those being corrected.

People tend to respond well to those who also encourage them on the path of life. As Charles Spurgeon has observed, "Blame comes best on the back of praise." So it is helpful to balance criticism and rebuke with words of encouragement, comfort, affirmation, praise, and hope.

> Before we offer any criticism, we should ask: Is it necessary that I comment critically about a certain person? Is it my place to criticize?

In keeping with this principle, Jesus often gives a commendation before a rebuke in his letters to the churches in Revelation.[16] Paul does the same in his epistles. After the stormy discipline and restoration of one rebellious member, he assures the believers in Corinth that he knew all along that they would do the right thing: "I have great pride in you; I am filled with comfort. In all our affliction, I am overflowing with joy. . . . I rejoice, because I have perfect confidence in you" (2 Cor. 7:4, 16).

e. Use Scripture to Instruct

All that we need for warning, correcting, and reproving others is provided in Scripture. Paul informs Timothy that "all Scripture" is "breathed out by God" and is useful for "reproof" and "correction" (2 Tim. 3:16). As we grow in our knowledge of Scripture, we are better able to rebuke and exhort "with complete patience and teaching" (2 Tim. 4:2). Scripture will also equip us personally for the task of correcting just as it equips us for "every good work" (2 Tim. 3:17).

---

[16]Rev. 2:1-3:22.

f. Welcome Criticism

Wise people recognize that they may be misguided or in error, so they welcome constructive criticism and correction. Proverbs repeatedly makes this point: "reprove a wise man, and he will love you. Give instruction to a wise man, and he will be still wiser; teach a righteous man, and he will increase in learning" (Prov. 9:8-9).[17]

Sadly, most of us take criticism and rebuke poorly. Because of our perverse pride, we are defensive and overly sensitive to criticism—even truthful, constructive criticism. But we can't change for the better or grow into Christlikeness without others correcting us. In affirmation of this principle, one Christian leader said to me, "My critics have been my best teachers."

If we need to criticize or rebuke others, it is important that we also are open to receiving rebuke and criticism. The psalmist David expresses beautifully the attitude of humility and wisdom with which we should welcome correction: "Let a righteous man strike me—it is a kindness; let him rebuke me—it is oil for my head; let my head not refuse it" (Ps. 141:5).

Let us not pass judgment on one another any longer.
Romans 14:13

Key Principles to Remember

1. When facing conflict, guard your tongue from speaking evil of others or being unduly critical.

2. Refrain from harsh, self-righteous, or unnecessary judgments of others.

3. Refrain from sinful grumbling and petty quarreling.

4. Criticize and rebuke according to biblical guidelines.

---

[17]Also Prov. 12:15; 13:10; 15:31; 17:10; 19:25; 25:12.

7

Pursue Reconciliation

If your brother sins against you, go and tell him his fault, between you and him alone. If he listens to you, you have gained your brother.
Matthew 18:15

When believers sin against one another, it causes conflict and estrangement. What are we to do when this happens? Run and join another church? Get on the phone and tell everyone how badly we have been treated? Recruit our friends and relatives to attack the person who has wronged us? Hold a grudge for the next twenty years? Hire the best lawyer and sue for all we can get?

We do none of the above.

Knowing that his followers would sin against one another and that broken relationships would need to be reconciled, Jesus gave specific instructions for dealing appropriately with personal offenses. Whether we have sinned against another person or have been sinned against, we are not to run and hide, nor are we to retaliate. Instead, we are to take the initiative to repair the relationship.

1. GO TO THE BROTHER *WHOM YOU HAVE OFFENDED*

If you know that a brother or sister in Christ has a legitimate complaint against you and is angry with you, you are to go to that person and reconcile. To make this point perfectly clear, Jesus says that if you remember a person who has something against you, you are to resolve the matter immediately. Even if you are engaged in the most solemn act of worship in the temple at Jerusalem, you must leave your sacrifice at the altar and resolve the matter:

> So if you are offering your gift at the altar and there remember
> that your brother has something against you, leave your gift

there before the altar and go. First be reconciled to your
brother, and then come and offer your gift. (Matt. 5:23-24)

Leon Morris comments on how important reconciliation is in Jesus'
teaching:

> The interruption of so solemn an act emphasizes the overriding
> importance of reconciliation. . . . He must take whatever steps
> are needed to restore harmony, and only when this is done
> may he come back and resume his offering.[1]

Clearly, trying to worship God when one's relationship with a brother
or sister is unreconciled is unacceptable to God.

John MacArthur notes that "reconciliation must precede
worship,"[2] but this principle often is not practiced. For example,
consider the conflict between Carl and Jim, two Christian businessmen
who attend the same church. Carl, an influential businessman in the
community, asks Jim, a building contractor, to put in the foundation
and frame a new house. When Jim's company finishes the job, he sends
Carl a bill. After waiting for months without payment, Jim calls Carl.
Carl doesn't return his phone calls. Jim's company is in financial straits,
and he needs the money to pay his employees. Finally, Carl tells Jim he
can't pay him because he, too, is experiencing economic problems.

A few weeks later, Jim finds out through an unusual series of
events that Carl has the money in his personal savings and investments
but that he doesn't want to use those funds. When Jim tells Carl what
he has discovered, Carl is outraged. He demands to know how Jim got
the information and refuses to pay Jim because he has pried into his
personal affairs.

At church, Carl sings in the choir and participates in a men's
Bible study, but he ignores Jim. He claims that Jim is unethical and
that their business deal went sour because of the economy. He seems
unconcerned about the Master's instructions regarding unreconciled

---

[1]Leon Morris, *The Gospel according to Matthew*, PNTC (Grand Rapids:
Eerdmans, 1992), 116.
[2]John MacArthur, *The MacArthur New Testament Commentary, Matthew 1-7*
(Chicago, IL: Moody, 1985), 296.

> Jesus places the responsibility for dealing with personal offenses on each individual.

relationships (Matt. 5:23-24). He seems to be unaware of his responsibility to take the initiative and go to Jim, whom he offended when he refused to pay. Carl also seems to be unaware that his worship is of little value to God because of the unconfessed sin and unresolved conflict with Jim.

2. GO TO THE BROTHER *WHO HAS SINNED AGAINST YOU*

Where does this leave Jim? What is he, or any believer, to do when a fellow believer sins against him? And what are we to do when another believer sins against us? The answer is found in our Lord's instruction in Matthew 18:15-17:

> "If your brother sins against you, go and tell him his fault, between you and him alone. If he listens to you, you have gained your brother. But if he does not listen, take one or two others along with you, that every charge may be established by the evidence of two or three witnesses. If he refuses to listen to them, tell it to the church. And if he refuses to listen even to the church, let him be to you as a Gentile and a tax collector." (Matt. 18:15-17)

Although this passage on dealing with sin and reconciliation is well known, it often is not practiced.

a. A Meeting Between Two Brothers

If a brother "sins against you"[3], you are to pursue reconciliation. You are not to wait for him to come to you. You are to go to him and point

---

[3]Some Greek manuscripts omit the phrase "against you." The UBS Greek New Testament places the words in square brackets indicting uncertainty. It doesn't matter much one way or the other. Even if the phrase be omitted, the instruction still applies to a brother sinning against a brother. See Matthew 18:21 and Luke 17:3-4.

out[4] the sin in an effort to "try to get the offender to see his sin for what it is."[5] Please note that the issue to be addressed is "sin," not a mere annoyance, petty grievance, or dislike of a fellow believer's appearance.

According to the passage, the offended believer is to go to the sinning believer and meet one-on-one. The purpose of this private meeting is to seek and to save, not to seek and to destroy. By making the meeting private, the sinning brother (or sister) is more easily won and protected from humiliation. The church family is spared involvement in the conflict, which helps to maintain peace and unity. (Just think how unpleasant a place the local church would be if every offense between brothers and sisters were brought out into the open!)

In direct violation of Jesus' teaching on private, face-to-face meetings between brothers or sisters, some Christians express their grievances against others over the Internet—using social networks, blogs, chat rooms, or even email. However, the Internet is no substitute for a face-to-face, private meeting in which one can see the other person's face, hear each other's voice, and witness the many subtleties of body language—all part of the mystery of personal presence. In the presence of another person, communication is enhanced and the other person does not come across as bad as he or she might seem in a flaming cyberspace rant.

If, as a result of this face-to-face meeting, the sinning brother sees his wrong and repents, Jesus says, "you have gained your brother." A victory has been won! A brother in Christ has been restored, sin has been dealt with properly, brothers are reconciled, Satan is defeated, church unity is preserved, and God is honored.

It is impossible to grasp the heartbeat of this passage unless we understand the theology of Christian brotherhood and sisterhood.[6] As

---

[4]"Tell him his fault" translates the Greek verb *elegchō*. France comments: "It is not easy to capture the force of *elegchō* here in a single English word. It includes the related ideas of reprimand, of bringing the wrong to light, of trying to bring the person to recognize that they are in the wrong, and of correcting them" (R.T. France, *Gospel of Matthew*, NICNT [Grand Rapids: Eerdmans, 2007], 689).
[5]Morris, *The Gospel according to Matthew*, 467.
[6]Heb. 2:10-12, 14,17; 13:1; 1 Peter 2:17. The term *brother* or *sister* (sisters are included in the term brothers) occurs approximately 250 times throughout the New Testament. The reality of this strong, familial community supersaturates the New Testament.

believers in Christ, we are members of the family of God—*real* brothers and sisters. We have the same heavenly Father and Elder Brother, the Lord Jesus Christ (Rom. 8:29). We share the same "life," given by the Holy Spirit. This eternal family relationship is stronger than any blood relationship.

This is why *Jesus places the responsibility for dealing with personal offenses on each individual member of the church community rather than on church "officials."* Believers are brothers and sisters in Christ and thus have the duty and right to speak to one another about offenses in order to reconcile family relationships that have been divided by sin. In our hypothetical situation between Jim and Carl, Jim would need to ask Carl to meet privately according to Matthew 18 in order to resolve the issue of nonpayment for work performed and to restore the unity of their relationship in Christ.

The purpose of this private meeting is to seek and to save, not to seek and to destroy.

——————— ❧ ———————

Jim and Carl get together, but the meeting does not go well. Carl focuses only on the fact that Jim has uncovered information about his personal finances, which he considers unethical. He accuses Jim of being a gossip and having sinned against him by telling other people about their financial disagreement. Jim insists that Carl has sinned against him by refusing to pay the bill when he had the money. Both men leave the meeting angry and frustrated. In Carl's mind, the matter is over and does not need to be pursued. What is Jim to do?

b. A Meeting Involving Witnesses

At this point, many people in Jim's position would give up and have nothing more to do with the offender. But in God's family, this is not acceptable. Sin must be dealt with; family relationships must be reconciled. So Jesus teaches that if you speak privately to a brother who has sinned against you and he will not listen to you, then a second step is to be taken (Matt. 18:15-16).

The second step is to go to the offender again, this time with one or two fellow believers as witnesses and mediators. Quoting from the Old Testament Scripture, Jesus says the purpose of the second meeting is "that every charge may be established by the evidence of two or three witnesses" (Matt. 18:16).[7] This small delegation is meant to keep the matter contained to a few people.

Whether or not these people are eyewitnesses of the offense (most likely they are not), they serve as witnesses to the offended believer's accusations and to the offender's responses. These witnesses are not passive observers. In an effort to win the erring member, they lend persuasiveness to the injured brother's appeal and make every effort to help the sinning brother listen and repent. They act as mediators and offer counsel, warning, and rebuke. They help to ensure justice and fairness for both individuals.

In the case of Carl and Jim, Jim asks another businessman in the church and one of the church elders to go with him to speak to Carl about the issue. At their second meeting, Jim again tells Carl that he is sinning by not paying his bill and by refusing to work out a payment plan. Carl responds by accusing Jim of being a whiner who does not understand that everyone in business takes losses. He again accuses Jim of malicious gossip and adds that Jim's work was substandard. At this false charge, Jim becomes very angry.

The two witnesses listen carefully without comment. Then they speak. Both witnesses agree that Carl has sinned against Jim by not paying the bill and that he is wrong in trying to excuse himself by finding fault with Jim. They also point out that Jim's employees are suffering as a result of Carl's failure to pay what he owes. They rebuke Carl for trying to transfer the blame to Jim and suggest that Carl lay out a plan for paying Jim as soon as possible.

Carl refuses, saying his business cannot pay the bill. At this point he becomes aggressive, claiming that he has been deeply hurt by all three men. He threatens to get a lawyer and sue for slander and emotional damages if they press the matter.

c. A Public Church Meeting

The next step in dealing with an unrepentant brother or sister is to take the matter to the church body, as Jesus directed. During this meeting the witnesses and the offended brother are to explain the details of the

---

[7]See also Deut. 19:15; Num. 35:30; 2 Cor. 13:1; 1 Tim. 5:19.

situation to the church body. Individual church members are then responsible to appeal to the sinning brother to repent.

If, after a specified period of time, the sinning brother does not listen to his brothers and sisters and stubbornly persists in sin, the final step is to be taken: The individual is to be treated as a "Gentile and a tax collector." The terms "Gentile" and "tax collector" are used here in the negative, conventional sense in which Jews in Jesus' day used them. Gentiles and tax collectors were excluded from the social life of devout Jews.

There are limits to what a church family can tolerate in regard to a member's blatant rebellion and sin. When a member is unrepentant and persists in sin, fellowship with that person is broken and he or she must be excluded from the church. Such severe discipline is intended to protect the local church from moral and spiritual corruption. It also awakens the sinner to the seriousness of his (or her) sin so that "his spirit may be saved in the day of the Lord" (1 Cor. 5:5).

This is the reasoning behind Paul's rebuke of the church in Corinth for its laxity toward the blatant sin of a member who is living in an illicit sexual relationship. Writing with full apostolic authority from Christ, Paul tells the church exactly what to do:

> But now I am writing to you *not to associate with* anyone who bears the name of brother if he is guilty of sexual immorality or greed, or is an idolater, reviler, drunkard, or swindler—*not even to eat with such a one.* For what have I to do with judging outsiders? Is it not those inside the church whom you are to judge? God judges those outside. *"Purge the evil person from among you."* (1 Cor. 5:11-13; italics added)

When Carl becomes even more obstinate after the second meeting, Jim takes the next step of confrontation. This takes courage and obedience because he knows that Carl will fight rather than give in. The two witnesses accompany Jim as he meets with the elders to apprise them of their conversation with Carl and his angry response. All agree that because Carl will not face his sin, the matter must be taken to the church body.

One of the elders calls Carl to tell him that they will call a special

Sunday night meeting to inform the church of his breach of good faith in his business dealings with Jim and of his rebellious attitude. The elder then pleads with Carl to change his attitude and correct his behavior. Carl, however, becomes verbally abusive. He says that his family and friends will be at the meeting to defend him. He again threatens a lawsuit if they make any public charges against him. He promises that there will be nothing left of the church when he is done with them.

Despite the possibility that Carl will sue and drag the church through an ugly court case, the elders decide that they must honor the Lord's instruction in Matthew 18. They announce that a discipline case will be presented on a Sunday evening and that all members need to attend. After opening the meeting with prayer, they set the tone for the meeting by reading aloud Matthew 18 and other portions of Scripture that address proper Christlike behavior and attitudes. They emphasize that the church is "God's temple and that God's Spirit dwells" in them (1 Cor 3:16). They remind the congregation that as a holy people they all must behave in a holy manner (1 Peter 1:15-16).

Following the opening prayers and exhortations regarding proper conduct and speech, Jim and the two witnesses present the issue. Questions and comments follow. As the evening progresses, it becomes obvious that Carl is wrong in not paying his bill and that his behavior and attitude toward his brothers are sinful. Carl doesn't speak, but some of his children speak on his behalf, echoing Carl's excuses and self-justification.

The congregation is then given two weeks to appeal to Carl to repent of his sin. During that time, Carl receives many caring phone calls and letters that ask him to change his stubborn behavior. Businessmen in the church even take him to lunch to reason with him, but Carl has already hired a lawyer to sue Jim and the church for slander and harassment.

Carl is invited to the next meeting. He does not attend, but his friends and relatives do. During the meeting the elders read Matthew 18 and 1 Corinthians 5. The church agrees that Carl is an unrepentant "reviler," "swindler," and "guilty of . . . greed" (1 Cor. 5:11-13), who must be put out of fellowship. The elders then allow time for questions regarding what exclusion from the congregation means in practical terms.

That week, Carl receives a letter and a visit from some of the elders telling him that he has been disfellowshipped but that he will be welcomed back with open arms and a joyful spirit if he repents. For now, however, they will have no social interaction with him and he is not welcome at the church. They also tell Carl that they will call to see if he would meet with some of them to pray and study God's Word in order to work toward his full restoration. Carl says, "See you in court."

d. Refusing Corrective Church Discipline

Many Christian believers will not follow the steps for dealing with unrepentant sin and for seeking reconciliation in the body of Christ. They refuse to practice official, corporate church discipline of an unrepentant member—even though Jesus instructs them to—because they find it too "harsh" or "unloving." Yet these same people may refuse to talk to or have anything to do with a brother or sister in Christ who has hurt their feelings. They will nurse a personal grudge against someone or even hate the person—the very thing Jesus forbids them to do. This is hypocrisy!

> "The judgment of the Church is the instrument of God's love, and the moment it is accepted in the sinful soul it begins to work as a redemptive force."
> —James Denny

The final step of corrective church discipline is particularly distasteful, in part because people have seen extremist sects and leaders abuse this text to punish godly people with whom they disagree. People may think that expulsion from a church is cruel and unloving, but such an attitude reflects the spirit of our age, not God's thinking. The fact is, every responsible sector of society—law enforcement, the military, legal and medical societies, the political and corporate worlds—has a code of discipline to protect itself from unlawful behavior among its members and to protect its integrity.

Sin must always be dealt with (both personally and corporately) otherwise it will spread like leaven and corrupt everything it touches.[8] So to ensure the moral purity of the church, God requires corrective church

---

[8]Old Testament scholar Derek Kidner, makes this insightful comment, "What an institution sometimes needs is not reforms, but the expulsion of a member; see Matthew 18:17" (*Proverbs*, TOTC [Downers Grove, IL: IVP, 1964], 148).

discipline. For the purpose of restoring a rebellious, impenitent sinner, God requires expulsion from the congregation. As James Denny writes, "The judgment of the Church is the instrument of God's love, and the moment it is accepted in the sinful soul it begins to work as a redemptive force."[9]

The Holy Spirit always leads believers to obey Christ's words. Practicing Matthew 5 and 18 is an example of what walking by the Spirit entails in practical, daily church life (Gal. 6:1). When we refuse to deal with sin and broken relationships, the problem only becomes worse. Moreover, when we refuse to deal with sin and rebellious, unrepentant members of the body, we walk in outright disobedience to our Lord's commands. Matthew's Gospel ends with the great commission (Matt. 28:19-20), part of which is to *teach new disciples to obey all that Jesus commanded.* This includes Matthew 5 and 18. To not teach and practice Matthew 5 and 18 is to disobey Christ's instruction.

3. GO IN THE RIGHT SPIRIT

When someone has sinned against us, the spirit of selfishness and pride says, "Let that person come to me. Let him humble himself before my feet. Let him plead for my forgiveness. It's *his* problem, not mine." Love, however, suffers long (1 Cor. 13:4). It seeks the good of the other person, even if he is in the wrong. It seeks to win the erring brother, not to crush him.

> **When we refuse to deal with sin and broken relationships, the problem only becomes worse.**

The New Testament emphasizes gentleness when dealing with people,[10] and when we are dealing with a brother or sister's sin, we are to be gentle, not harsh or arrogant. Paul, for example, appeals to the wayward Corinthians "by the meekness and gentleness of Christ" (2 Cor. 10:1). To the Galatians Paul writes, "Brothers, if anyone is caught in any transgression, you who are spiritual should restore him in a spirit of gentleness" (Gal. 6:1).

So, when we approach an offending or offended brother, we

---

[9]James Denny, *The Second Epistle to the Corinthians*, The Expositor's Bible (New York: Funk & Wagnalls, 1900), 75.
[10]See also 1 Cor. 4:21; 2 Cor. 10:1; Eph. 4:1-2; 1 Thess. 2:7; 1 Tim. 3:3; 6:11; 2 Tim. 2:24-25; Titus 3:2; Heb. 5:2; James 3:17; 1 Peter 3:15-16.

will want to conduct ourselves in a manner that is likely to win him over rather than to put him off. Actions that are motivated by love, gentleness, and forgiveness tend to build up a relationship rather than tear it down. If the principles of love, gentleness, and forgiveness govern our actions and attitudes during a confrontation with a fellow believer, we greatly increase the likelihood of a favorable outcome.

One reason people often avoid confronting sin is because they don't want to be party to the damage that is done by harsh, angry confrontations. But confrontation doesn't have to be ugly or hurtful.

When confrontation is done in the power of the Holy Spirit with gentleness and tact, it can be cathartic and life-saving. When we seek to address broken relationships in the body of Christ, we must be willing to offer forgiveness freely. Forgiveness is a paramount Christian virtue that represents the very heart of the gospel.[11] The New Testament expresses clearly God's standard for forgiveness:

- And forgive us our debts, as we also have forgiven our debtors . . . . for if you forgive others their trespasses, your heavenly Father will also forgive you, but if you do not forgive others their trespasses, neither will your Father forgive your trespasses. (Matt. 6:12, 14-15)

- And whenever you stand praying, forgive, if you have anything against anyone, so that your father also who is in heaven may forgive you your trespasses. (Mark 11:25)

- Pay attention to yourselves! If your brother sins, rebuke him, and if he repents, forgive him, and if he sins against you seven times in the day, and turns to you seven times, saying, 'I repent,' you must forgive him. (Luke 17:3-4)

- Forgiving one another, as God in Christ forgave you. (Eph. 4:32)

- Bearing with one another and, if one has a complaint against another, forgiving each other; as the Lord has forgiven you, so you also must forgive. (Col. 3:13)

---

[11]Matt. 6:12-15; Luke 17:3-4; Eph. 4:32; Col. 3:13; 2 Cor. 2:7, 10.

- So you should rather turn to forgive and comfort him, or he may be overwhelmed by excessive sorrow [a sinning brother who repented after being disciplined]. (2 Cor. 2:7)

Our heavenly Father has forgiven each of us a debt we could never pay. How, then, can we refuse to forgive a fellow believer who sins against us? Unforgiveness is a most serious sin with dire consequences. When Jesus tells the parable of the unforgiving servant, he warns: "So also my heavenly Father will do to every one of you [speaking of severe punishment], if you do not forgive your brother from your heart" (Matt. 18:35).

Without forgiveness, we cannot put our conflicts behind us and live together in harmony. So we must be prepared to graciously and repeatedly forgive those who repent after sinning against us.[12] And when we offend someone in the body of Christ, we must be willing to confess our sin and ask for forgiveness.

Having a spirit of love, gentleness, and forgiveness when we are dealing with the sins and offenses of our fellow believers can make a huge difference in their response. In the case of Jim and Carl, Jim was consistently gracious. He prayed for the Lord to help him act in love and display the fruit of the Spirit. When he called to request payment, he approached his brother with a spirit of gentleness and understanding. The witnesses who assisted him also were gentle yet firm. The ensuing church discipline was handled with love and truth. Individual members of the body demonstrated sincere concern for Carl. They were eager to forgive and receive Carl back into fellowship if he would repent.

> "Let each one of you speak the truth with his neighbor, for we are members one of another."
> Ephesians 4:25

4. SPEAK THE TRUTH IN LOVE AND WITH COURAGE

When we become a new person in Christ, we "put away falsehood,"

---

[12]For help in understanding some of the difficult questions regarding forgiveness, see Chris Brauns, *Unpacking Forgiveness: Biblical Answers for Complex Questions and Deep Wounds* (Wheaton, IL: Crossway, 2008).

lies (including white lies), deception, and half-truths. Furthermore, we become "members one of another" in the body of Christ (Eph. 4:25). So the local church is to be a community in which people speak the truth to one another: "Let each one of you speak the truth with his neighbor, for we are members one of another" (Eph. 4:25). Lying to one another undermines our very identity in Christ and our unique, Spirit-formed relationships with other believers.

Christ's instructions in Matthew 5 and 18 remind us that we must speak the truth in love and with courage. Although telling the truth may create conflict in the short term, it is best for the long-term health and unity of the church. "Speaking the truth in love" is essential to our growth—as individuals and as a body—into Christlikeness (Eph. 4:15).

a. Speaking the Truth

As believers, we are to have the same regard for the truth that God does: "Behold, you delight in truth in the inward being" (Ps. 51:6). If a believer who is sinned against denies that any offense has taken place, then it is a lie. But an offended believer who gently approaches the offending believer about the offense acts according to truth. If a believer who is confronted with sin denies it, then it is a lie—to the believer, to other believers, and to God. But a believer who confesses or confronts his or her sin walks in the truth.

Unfortunately, we often prefer a comforting lie over the challenging truth. In fact, when Paul confronted the Galatians who were being misled by false teachers, he boldly challenged them to face the truth: "Have I then become your enemy by telling you the truth?" (Gal. 4:16). Paul could not flatter the Galatians as the false teachers did. He loved them and told them the truth about their sad spiritual condition. Although they did not want to hear it, Paul's compassionate truth-telling rescued them from the death grip of a false gospel.

b. Speaking with Courage

Most people fear confrontation, and in many cultures approaching another person to correct sin or to seek reconciliation is to be avoided at all costs. Consequently, it can be difficult for us to obey Christ's instruction to "go and tell him his fault, between you and him alone" (Matt. 18:15). But the principles of Matthew 5 and 18 transcend culture and apply universally to the body of Christ. Like many of Christ's teachings, these principles are counterintuitive and countercultural.[13] Practicing them will take courage regardless of our personal experiences and cultural expectations.

It takes courage to take the initiative, to speak the truth in love, to stand against culture, or to face an angry person who refuses correction. Thankfully, we can have courage through the power of the Holy Spirit whom God has put within us to help us understand and do his will. Walking by the Spirit gives us the courage to confront sin by speaking the truth in love.

c. Hope for Reconciliation

If we stand on truth and act in love as we seek to deal with personal offenses, there is real hope for reconciliation, healing, and peace in our relationships with other believers. Consider, for example, the outcome of the church discipline case described earlier in this chapter. For a while, things seemed only to get worse. Carl hired a lawyer to sue the church for slander. Due to a lack of evidence, the lawyer dropped the case. This only made Carl angrier. He told everyone who would listen that the church was a cult and that he had been abused by it.

> Although telling the truth may create conflict in the short term, it is best for the long-term health and unity of the church.

Carl insisted that Jim had sinned against him and that the elders mishandled the discipline. His adult children, however, began to realize that they had been wrong to go along with their father's lies. They felt that their relationship with the Lord had been adversely affected by the situation. Rather than continue to be complicit in their father's sins, they respectfully confronted him together.

Motivated by true love for their father, Carl's children told him that they were going to go back to the church to ask for forgiveness

---

[13]Matt. 5:3, 5, 11-12, 21, 27, 31, 33, 38-48; 6:1-4, 19-21, 24-34; 7:1-5; 10:37-38; 15:11, 18; 18:2-4, 15, 21-35; 22:37-39; 23:5-12.

for the sins they had committed while defending him. They recognized that their family and the church had been hurt by their father's sinful actions and attitudes. They said that they needed to stand against his self-destructive, sinful behavior and hoped that he would confess his sins and reconcile with them and the church.

Carl was shocked by his children's words, but they had a profound effect on him. Months passed as the Holy Spirit worked on his conscience. Finally he requested a meeting with the elders. They had been praying for him regularly and responded to his request with joy.

It takes courage to take the initiative, to speak the truth in love, to stand against culture, or to face an angry person who refuses correction.

At their meeting, Carl reluctantly admitted that he had acted "inappropriately," which was woefully inadequate and caused the elders to question whether Carl recognized the severity of his behavior. Concerned that Carl might be whitewashing his sin, the elders asked him to specify what sins he was confessing. At first, Carl was uncomfortable verbalizing his sins, but he saw that the elders were resolved not to go forward until he clearly stated his sins and whom he had sinned against. During the course of the conversation, the elders saw Carl become repentant about the reality of his sins. They all prayed together and embraced each other in a time of tearful rejoicing.

Afterward, Carl voluntarily repaid his debt to Jim. He was joyfully welcomed back into the church family. He took extra steps to renew his friendships with some of the elders, inviting them out for lunch or dinner and expressing his deep love and respect for them and their courage to stand up to his willful and rebellious deception. In the end, the outcome of the entire disciplinary process was a victory for the truth of the gospel.

So if you are offering your gift at the altar and there remember that your brother has something against you, leave your gift there before the altar and go. First be reconciled to your brother, and then come and offer your gift.
Matthew 5:23-24

Key Principles to Remember

1. Take the initiative to reconcile broken relationships whenever an offense occurs. Whether someone has sinned against you, or you have sinned against another person, take the initiative to reconcile the relationship.

2. Practice Matthew 5 and 18 by going first to the sinning member privately. If that does not work, go with one or two witnesses. If that does not work, bring the matter to the church body for the purpose of repentance and restoration of the relationship.

3. Always speak the truth in love.

4. Be ready to forgive and to ask for forgiveness.

8

Pursue Peace

Let us pursue what makes for peace and for mutual upbuilding.
Romans 14:19

Imagine Grace Church, a missionary-planted church that from its earliest days had been a contentious group. Personality clashes among prominent families and factions that formed around differing doctrinal perspectives had often disrupted its unity and peace. It was, in many ways, like the first-century church in Corinth. The people had remained in fellowship together primarily because they lived in a country where Christians were a small minority and there were few other churches from which to choose.

For many months the church had been engaged in a particularly rancorous fight over differing views regarding the dates of creation. It looked like the church was about to break apart. Then, to everyone's surprise, one of the deacons stood up at the end of the Sunday service and addressed the congregation.

In gentle tones he expressed his frustration with the sinful attitudes and behaviors that had become standard practice when dealing with any matter of controversy in the church. Worst of all, not one person, the deacon pointed out, had yet made an effort at peacemaking. With great courage he quoted Galatians 5:15 from memory: "If you bite and devour one another, watch out that you are not consumed by one another." No one could deny that these words spoke directly to their church; they were about to consume one another through their bitter debates.

The congregation's response was overwhelmingly positive. Everyone had been hurt by the angry words and distorted accusations. They were exhausted by the constant conflict. They knew something had to be done and recognized the Spirit's leading through this deacon's humble exhortation.

When he finished speaking, others began to offer suggestions for how the church might rediscover the blessed state of peace that God intended them to enjoy together. One suggested that Sunday mornings

107

be devoted to teaching on the major peacemaking passages in the Bible. Another suggested meeting in small groups on Sunday nights to review the sermon and to prayerfully apply the Scriptures to the problems they faced. After two months of listening to messages on peacemaking and individually studying the biblical passages on peace, the congregation identified seven key concepts that they needed to understand and implement if their church was to experience peace and unity.

1. PEACEMAKING IS BLESSED BY THE LORD JESUS CHRIST

In 1895, Alfred Nobel willed a portion of his personal fortune to award people who make peace. But long before this war-torn world began selecting individuals to win the famed Nobel Peace Prize, Jesus announced the blessedness of peacemaking. In his Sermon on the Mount, Jesus gave peacemakers far superior recognition: "Blessed are the peacemakers, for they shall be called sons of God" (Matt. 5:9).

"This beatitude," explains David Turner, "is not about being a passively peaceful person but about being an active reconciler of people."[1] When Jesus said, "Blessed are the peacemakers," he was not referring to those who merely *keep peace*. He was referring to those who *make peace*—those "who end hostilities and bring the quarrelsome together."[2]

Jesus' simple words reveal that peacemaking is Godlike work that is blessed by God. In fact, Scripture tells us that God is the "God of peace,"[3] and the cross is his paramount peacemaking work![4] Since our Father in heaven takes peacemaking seriously, we also should take it seriously. As his children, we should be peacemakers whose thoughts and actions reflect our Father's character and work, especially when it comes to handling conflict.

As the congregation at Grace Church began to recognize the

---

[1] David L. Turner, *Matthew*, BECNT (Grand Rapids: Baker, 2008), 152.
[2] Leon Morris, *The Gospel according to Matthew* (Grand Rapids: Eerdmans, 1992), 101.
[3] Rom. 15:33; 16:20; 2 Cor. 13:11; Phil. 4:9; 1 Thess. 5:23; 2 Thess. 3:16; Heb. 13:20.
[4] Eph. 2:14-17; Col. 1:19-20.

depth of God's commitment to peacemaking, a new awareness dawned upon their collective conscience. They admitted, to their shame, that they had never even prayed for the peace of their church! They had become skilled at arguing and fighting over topics of special interest but lacked any ability to wage peace in their relationships with one another or in their community.

Their study of biblical peacemaking led them to begin thinking and acting as peacemakers and not troublemakers. Real changes started to occur in how they approached their differences and related to one another. Jesus' words to his disciples rang with fresh, new meaning in their ears: "Blessed are the peacemakers, for they shall be called sons of God."

2. PEACEMAKING PRODUCES HEALTHY, SANCTIFIED LIVES AND CHURCHES

Grace Church members were continually challenged by what they were learning from Scripture. One sermon was particularly helpful. It focused on James 3:18, where James praises "those who make peace" for the benefits they contribute to the believing community:

> But the wisdom from above is first pure, then peaceable. . . .
> And a harvest of righteousness is sown in peace by those who
> make peace. (James 3:17-18)

As a student of the Old Testament, James knew the Jewish concept of *shalom*, or peace, that denotes "wholeness" and "well-being" both in the inner life of the self and outward life of the community. *Shalom* conveys not just the absence of fighting, but the positive qualities of contentment, security, and prosperity. It is peace with God, with one's state of mind (inner tranquility), with one's fellow creatures (group harmony), and with one's enemies (cessation of war).

God is the source of *shalom*, and his peace is to be one of the great blessings his people enjoy. James wanted these first Jewish Christian congregations, which were experiencing anything but peace, to truly experience *shalom*. So, using a farming image, he likened peacemakers to farmers who sow seed and look forward to harvesting a valuable crop.

Unlike farmers who sow seeds in the ground, peacemakers sow seeds in the minds and hearts of their fellow believers. They sow seeds "in peace," not in anger, or out of selfishness, or with impatience. In time, the seeds they have sown produce a crop—a blessed harvest of sanctified lives and churches. The "harvest of righteousness" that peacemaking believers produce is godly, righteous conduct that pleases God—conduct that is "pure . . . peaceable, gentle, open to reason, full of mercy and good fruits, impartial and sincere" (v. 17). It is conduct that reflects the "fruit of the Spirit" and Christlike behavior. It is conduct that maintains harmony among people.

Peace is absolutely essential to the spiritual health of a local church and to an individual's growth in sanctification. In an environment of warfare and contending factions, spiritual growth is stifled. Where there is discord, fear and distrust abound; frustration, anger, and distress fill the hearts of the people. In such an atmosphere, the gospel witness is hindered and new believers and children become disillusioned. In contrast, people—especially new believers and young people—thrive spiritually in an environment of peace. Where there is peace they can develop their spiritual gifts, serve others, grow into maturity, and experience the wonderful joy of the Lord.

> Peace is absolutely essential to the spiritual health of a local church and to an individual's growth in sanctification.

In a world of constant warfare is it any wonder that the psalmist cries out from the depth of his being, "Behold, how good and pleasant it is when brothers dwell in unity" (Ps. 133:1)? May we all share the psalmist's passion for peace and unity among God's people.

3. PEACEMAKING IS EVERY BELIEVER'S RESPONSIBILITY

As they continued their study of Scripture, the members of Grace Church were surprised to discover that peacemaking is not optional; it is a biblical command. The New Testament calls for all believers to live in peace with one another and with all people:

- Be at peace with one another. (Mark 9:50)

- If possible, so far as it depends on you, live peaceably with all. (Rom. 12:18)

- Live in peace [with one another]. (2 Cor. 13:11)

- Be at peace among yourselves. (1 Thess. 5:13)

Furthermore, they learned that all believers—not just those in positions of leadership—are called to intentionally and actively pursue peace:

- Let us pursue what makes for peace. (Rom. 14:19)

- Strive for peace with everyone. (Heb. 12:14)

- Let him seek peace and pursue it. (1 Peter 3:11)

- So flee youthful passions and pursue . . . peace. (2 Tim. 2:22)

- Let the peace of Christ rule in your hearts, to which indeed you were called in one body. (Col. 3:15)

"Peace," both in individual hearts and the church community, is a fruit of the Holy Spirit and is the antithesis of the works of the flesh, which are, "enmity, strife . . . rivalries, dissensions, divisions" (Gal. 5:20). Peace, not warfare, is to characterize our relationships as members of the "one body." As Colossians 3:15 points out, we have been called by God to let Christ's peace rule in our lives as we relate to one another since we are "one body" in Christ. "Without sacrificing principle," writes Douglas Moo, "believers should relate to one another in a way that facilitates and demonstrates the peace that Christ has secured for them."[5]

Each member, then, is responsible for the peace and unity of the local church. Each individual makes a difference as to the outcome of

---

[5]Douglas J. Moo, *The Letter to the Colossians and to Philemon*, PNTC (Grand Rapids: Eerdmans, 2008), 283.

any conflict in the church. Believers are, as one commentator concludes, "God's own 'peace corps.'"[6]

The New Testament teaches, and most Christians know, that every member of the local church family is responsible for encouraging, praying for, exhorting, serving, admonishing, teaching, building up, caring for, and loving one another. But, it seems, it is not well known that each member is also to "pursue what makes for peace" (Rom. 14:19). Imagine what it would be like to be part of a church in which every member thinks of himself or herself as one of God's own "peace corps." Each member would face conflict by thinking and acting as a peacemaker. Each would work for a just and righteous peace rather than competing against one another to win a fight or to beat down the opposing party.

Peacemaking is active, necessary work that demands deliberate thought and effort. Every church in the New Testament struggled with maintaining unity and harmony. It is no different today. Without constant peacemaking efforts, all churches will eventually break apart or live in perpetual warfare. Handling conflict biblically, then, requires all believers—leaders as well as followers (1 Thess. 5:13)—to think and act as peacemakers.

4. PEACEMAKING REQUIRES MEDIATION

At the end of the preaching series on biblical peacemaking at Grace Church, one of the teachers called upon all the members to begin to act as gospel peacemakers. To help remedy the hostilities within the congregation, he called upon the more mature believers to act as mediators among those who no longer spoke to one another. He reminded them that as Spirit-indwelt believers armed with God's Word, they should be able to help their

Each member is responsible for the peace and unity of the local church. Each individual makes a difference as to the outcome of any conflict in the church.

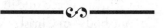

---

[6]William Hendriksen, *Exposition of the Gospel According to Matthew*, NTC (Grand Rapids: Baker Book House, 1973), 279.

brothers and sisters resolve most of their disputes.[7] He then explained three key New Testament passages on peacemaking: Matthew 18:15-17; Philippians 4:2-3; and 1 Corinthians 6:1-11.

a. Call on a Mediator for Help

By following our Lord's instructions, believers should be able to resolve personal conflicts with the help of fellow believers. The first step, according to Matthew 18:15-17, is to meet privately with the offending believer to resolve the conflict. If the offending individual will not cooperate, then we are to take another person or two as witnesses (refer to chapter 7 for a detailed examination of this process). One duty of the witnesses is to help mediate between the two individuals.

Even the most godly, dedicated Christians at times need help to resolve their disputes with one another. Paul, for example, was a tireless peacemaker. His letter to the church at Philippi was an effort to help a church in conflict. He specifically addressed two prominent women in the church who were caught up in conflict:

> I entreat Euodia and I entreat Syntyche to agree in the Lord. Yes, I ask you also, true companion, help these women, who have labored side by side with me in the gospel. (Phil. 4:2-3)

These women needed a mediator to step in to help them reconcile their differences. So Paul called on an unnamed believer in the congregation to get involved and help these godly women "to agree in the Lord." As long as people are in conflict, they will need mediating peacemakers.

b. Call on the Church Body for Wisdom and Help

It appears that one believer in the church at Corinth swindled or cheated another of money, property, or wages. To resolve the dispute, the Christian who was "wronged" (the plaintiff) took the Christian who presumably cheated (the defendant) to court. When Paul heard of this

---

[7]Mediation is a voluntary agreement between conflicting parties and is not binding, as opposed to arbitration, which results in a mandated and legally binding settlement.

situation, he was appalled. In disbelief he exclaimed: "Brother goes to law against brother, and that before unbelievers?" (1 Cor. 6:6). David Garland captures Paul's abhorrence of the situation: "Brother Christians are pitted against brother Christians, adopting a cutthroat, adversarial relationship rather than one based on love and selflessness."[8]

Paul sharply rebuked their willingness to seek the help of outsiders in settling internal disputes. In effect he asks, "Are you incompetent to try trivial cases? Can it be that no one among you is wise enough to settle a dispute between brothers?" In view of the fact that the saints will one day judge the world and angels, Paul sees the case at hand as a trivial matter that the church should be able to judge.

Furthermore, he asserts that, "to have lawsuits at all with one another is already a defeat for you" (1 Cor. 6:7). To Paul, taking a fellow believer before unbelievers for judgment is a complete spiritual and moral defeat for both parties—no matter who wins or loses. The one who defrauds is wrong, the one who takes the cheater to court is wrong, and the church is wrong for not stopping such a violation of Christian brotherhood and sisterhood.

One reason we see a proliferation of lawsuits among believers in certain Western countries is that local churches are not teaching or modeling Christian mediation as they should. Problems that are reminiscent of the situation in Corinth actually stem from deeply rooted spiritual issues that no court of law can resolve. Christians can hire the best lawyers money can afford, try their disputes in court, and receive a judgment made by an expert judge without ever addressing their hate, anger, self-righteousness, or pride. The problem is not insufficient arbitration or a lack of professional litigation. The real problem with resolution through the courts is a spiritual problem: fleshly desires still dominate our hearts and minds and have not been honestly faced or repented of before a holy God.

So the first order of peacemaking is to examine and deal with sinful attitudes of the heart. In the words of our Lord,

> For from within, out of the heart of man, come evil thoughts
> . . . envy, slander, pride, foolishness. All these evil things
> come from within, and they defile a person. (Mark 7:21-23)

---

[8]David E. Garland, *1 Corinthians*, BECNT (Grand Rapids: Baker, 2003), 208.

5. PEACEMAKING IS COURAGEOUS, HARD WORK

Many of the believers at Grace Church confessed that they viewed peacemakers as compromisers, cowards, and weaklings. But they came to understand that Christian peacemaking is not about ignoring problems, wishing that they would go away, or negotiating a truce. It is not appeasement or peace at any price. Christian peacemaking is hard, sacrificial work that must be guided by the truths of Scripture.

Paul's life provides a model of Christian peacemaking. He recognized the gospel as both "the word of truth" and "the gospel of peace" (Eph. 1:13; 6:15). When compromise was an acceptable course of action to help believers live together in harmony, he was ready and willing to compromise.[9] But when the truths of the gospel and God's Word were at stake, Paul would not compromise the truth or appease anyone, even friends.[10] He would not yield an inch of ground to the enemies of the gospel.

Paul understood that peace and unity cannot exist apart from the truth of the gospel. To compromise the gospel of truth would be to lose what creates our unity and peace:

> *When a decision must be made between unity and truth, unity must yield to truth; for it is better to be divided by truth than to be united by error.* We test the church by truth, not truth by the church. The apostles judged the Christian community by the norm of divine revelation.[11]

Like his Lord, Paul faced sin squarely. He didn't sweep problems and sins under the rug and declare peace when there was no peace. He took peace-breaking sins seriously.

When Jesus cleansed the temple and drove out the moneychangers, he brought peace to the temple worship. He reestablished spiritual well-being and wholeness to the covenant people of God (John 2:13-17). In a similar way, Paul often engaged in conflict

---

[9]Acts 16:3; 21:20-26; 24:17-18; 1 Cor. 9:20-23.
[10]Acts 15:1-2; Gal. 2:4-5; 11-14.
[11]Edward John Carnell, *The Case for Biblical Christianity* (Grand Rapids: Eerdmans, 1969), 27.

with false teachers who were sowing discord and division among God's people. When Paul and Barnabas resisted false teachers who began teaching a law-centered gospel in the new church in Antioch, for example, they and the apostles and elders of Jerusalem made a united, written declaration of Gentile freedom from Jewish law keeping (Acts 15:1-2, 6-35). Their efforts to stop false teaching brought peace and well-being to the churches (Acts 15:31).

> "When a decision must be made between unity and truth, unity must yield to truth; for it is better to be divided by truth than to be united by error."
> —Edward John Carnell

As one who labored sacrificially for truth and peace, Paul knew well the personal, painful cost of establishing and maintaining true peace in a hostile world. Paul Rees describes Paul's attitude toward peacemaking this way: "When unity was broken, his heart broke with it. When unity was strengthened his soul sang."[12]

6. PEACEMAKING PRIZES THE UNITY OF THE BODY OF CHRIST

Although peacemaking is difficult work—emotionally, mentally, and spiritually—the sacrifices we make for peace will never match the infinite price Christ paid to establish the new humanity of Jew and Gentile united as one in his body (Eph. 2:11-22). As the members of Grace Church began to grasp the magnitude of the unifying, peacemaking work Christ accomplished upon the cross, they began in a new way to prize unity and the work of peacemaking. This desire is what our Lord had prayed for just hours before his death. He prayed for all his people to become one and for that oneness to be visibly displayed to the world:

> I do not ask for these only, but also for those who will believe in me through their word, that they may all be one, just as you, Father, are in me, and I in you, that they also may be in us, so that the world may believe that you have sent me. The

---

[12]Paul S. Rees, *The Adequate Man: Paul in Philippians* (Westwood, NJ: Revell, 1959), 40.

glory that you have given me I have given to them, that they may be one even as we are one, I in them and you in me, that they may become perfectly one. (John 17:20-23)

So important is this oneness that Paul pleads with Gentile and Jewish believers who faced social tensions between themselves to be "eager to maintain the unity of the Spirit in the bond of peace" (Eph. 4:3). The Greek word for "eager" is a strong word that can be translated "make every effort," "strive," "be zealous," "be diligent," or be "conscientious."[13] Paul reminded these believers that

There is one body and one Spirit—just as you were called to the one hope that belongs to your call—one Lord, one faith, one baptism, one God and Father of all, who is over all and through all and in all. (Eph. 4:4-6)

Paul is not exhorting believers to create unity. The unity that Paul speaks of is the one body of Christ, the church. It is created by the Holy Spirit, not by us. Our calling is to preserve, protect, and maintain the unity that already exists. We are to spare no effort to "maintain" in practical and visible ways the "unity of the Spirit." We must do so with diligence and urgency because this unity is always at risk of attack. Every church in the New Testament struggled with preserving "the unity of the Spirit."

The virtues, or the types of conduct, necessary to preserve and protect the glorious unity of the Spirit are described in verse 2:

Walk in a manner worthy of the calling to which you have been called, with all *humility* and *gentleness*, with *patience*, *bearing with one another in love*. (Eph. 4:1-2; italics added)

7. VIRTUES OF PEACEMAKING

Preserving and protecting "the unity of the Spirit in the bond of

---

[13]"Eager," *spoudazō*: "be zealous/eager, take pains, make every effort, be conscientious" (BDAG, 939).

peace" is peacemaking work. How we do this work is clearly prescribed in God's Word. *It is to be done in a distinctly Christian way* "with all humility and gentleness, with patience, bearing with one another in love."[14] These virtues are fruits of the Spirit and without these Christlike qualities, we could not preserve and protect "the unity of the Spirit" or act as "God's own peace corps."

We cannot maintain "the unity of the Spirit" by acting harshly or arrogantly with people; we cannot preserve "the unity of the Spirit" with an impatient or a judgmental spirit of self-superiority and contempt for others, or a lack of compassion. These are works of the flesh and lead only to strife and division. It matters a great deal to God how we treat people.

Christlike peacemakers, then, humbly put the good of others ahead of themselves. They deal with difficult people with a gentle voice and hand. They act in love by denying themselves in order to solve problems and unite God's people. They deal patiently with people, bearing with them in love.[15]

Christlike, Spirit-led peacemakers control the destructive passions of anger and the untameable tongue so that they can speak with grace and truth to bring justice, healing, and unity to people in conflict. They display good listening skills and self-forgetfulness.

Spirit-guided peacemakers act in faithfulness to the truths of the gospel and the Word of God. They balance truth and graciousness in their dealings with people and their problems. They exhibit the wisdom from above, which produces purity of heart and mind, sweet reasonableness, graciousness, mercy, sincerity, and peace.

George Verwer, the founder and former director of Operation Mobilization, a worldwide mission organization, speaks in hundreds of churches in any given year. When asked what he has observed in the churches he visits all over the world, he said, "To see a church at peace is an oasis in the desert." What a commentary on the work of Christian

---

[14]See also Colossians 3:12-15.

[15]F. J. A. Hort comments about Paul that, "in each of the nine Epistles addressed to [the churches] he makes the *peace* of God to be the supreme standard for them to aim at, and the perpetual self-surrender of love the comprehensive means of attaining it" (*The Christian Ecclesia* [1897; repr. ed. London: Macmillan, 1914], 123).

peacemaking! We have much work to do!

Over time, Grace Church caught the biblical vision of peacemaking. It still had much to learn and accomplish, but its members were determined, by the Spirit's help, to change their quarrelsome, factious ways. They were making a diligent effort to "maintain the unity of the Spirit in the bond of peace." They were becoming a church at peace, an oasis in the desert. May your church also seek to become an oasis.

> *Agree with one another, live in peace; and the God of love and peace*
> *will be with you.*
> 2 Corinthians 13:11

Key Principles to Remember

1. When in conflict, every believer is to intentionally and actively pursue peacemaking.

2. When in conflict, seek help and mediation from the church body, not secular courts.

3. Make every effort to preserve and protect "the unity of the Spirit in the bond of peace."

9

Face False Teachers

If anyone teaches a different doctrine and does not agree with the sound words of our Lord Jesus Christ . . . he is puffed up with conceit. . . . He has an unhealthy craving for controversy and for quarrels about words, which produce envy, dissension, slander, evil suspicions, and constant friction among people. . . .
1 Timothy 6:3-5

Motivated by Satan and his demonic forces,[1] false teachers have been creating counterfeit gods and theologies from the dawn of human history. Paul warns that false teachers "cause divisions."[2] Jude puts it this way: "It is these who cause divisions, worldly people, devoid of the Spirit" (Jude 19). False teachers are wolves who scatter and devour the flock.

What are believers to do when false teachers attack their congregations? We might be tempted to run away from them, to make concessions so that we might work together in unity, to embrace them as brothers, to engage them in debate, or to remain silent and wait for God's intervention. But for the right answer, we must look to God's Word. For our protection, the Scriptures provide specific instructions for how to deal with false teachers—masterminds of confusion and conflict. Dealing with false teachers of the gospel is quite different from dealing with legitimate disagreements among fellow believers in the church family. So let us explore the specific New Testament directives on this subject.

In order to better understand the insidious nature of false teachers and to illustrate the process of faithfully and practically applying New Testament teaching to the problem, we will use the fictional example of Wolfgang, a German missionary to India. Wolfgang was a large-hearted, gracious man who had a special gift for mastering languages and adapting to other cultures. People loved him, and new believers

---

[1] 2 Cor. 11:3, 13-15; Eph. 6:11-12; 1 Tim. 4:1-2.
[2] Rom. 16:17; also Jude 19; 1 Tim. 6:4; Titus 1:11; 3:9.

in India eagerly followed his example of evangelism, which led to the formation of many new churches.

After years of hard work, Wolfgang returned to Germany for rest and medical attention. While he was away, missionaries from other parts of India visited the new churches. Some of them were compelling speakers—more so than Wolfgang—but these teachers proclaimed a false gospel. Although Wolfgang had repeatedly and sternly warned the churches of the threat of false teachers, the believers did not take his warnings to heart. They did not realize that the visiting teachers had come to wreak havoc in the newly formed churches.

1. WARN ALL BELIEVERS ABOUT FALSE TEACHERS

During his earthly ministry, Jesus, the Good Shepherd, repeatedly warned his followers about the pernicious teachings and subtle methods of false teachers.[3] "Beware of false prophets, who come to you in sheep's clothing but inwardly are ravenous wolves" (Matt. 7:15). The New Testament writers continued this theme by offering relentless warnings about false teachers and their destructive doctrines.

To his beloved converts in the city of Philippi, Paul declares: "For many, of whom I have often told you and now tell you even with tears, walk as enemies of the cross of Christ" (Phil. 3:18). Peter also warns "there will be false teachers among you, who will secretly bring in destructive heresies. . . . And in their greed they will exploit you with false words" (2 Peter 2:1, 3). And John warns his readers to not be gullible: "Beloved, do not believe every spirit, but test the spirits to see whether they are from God, for many false prophets have gone out into the world" (1 John 4:1). Their message is clear: Believers need continual warnings to guard against the subtle deceptions of false teachers.

Perhaps the most ominous warning regarding false teachers is found in Paul's farewell speech to the Ephesian elders:

> I know that after my departure fierce wolves will come in
> among you, not sparing the flock; and from among your own
> selves will arise men speaking twisted things, to draw away the

[3]Matt. 7:15; 16:6, 11-12; 24:5, 11, 23-24; Mark 8:15; 13:22; Luke 6:26; 12:1.

disciples after them. Therefore be alert, remembering that for three years I did not cease night or day to admonish everyone with tears. (Acts 20:29-31)

False teachers are not caricatures of little red devils with horned heads. They are real people. Some appear as distinguished professors at prestigious universities, as authors of scholarly books, or as popular speakers with revolutionary ideas. Still others appear as pastors of influential churches. Most often, false teachers are charming, intelligent, and likeable. They appear "as apostles of Christ" or "as an angel of light" (2 Cor. 11:13-14), but their teachings reveal that they are not. They create chaos and conflict among God's people. They mislead millions of people by cleverly redefining the Christian faith in a way that denies the essential, foundational truths of the gospel. Such teachers cannot be accommodated or compromised with in any way.

It is easier than one might think to be deceived by false teachers. They are masters at mixing precious truth and egregious error in ways that are difficult even for scholars to untangle. This is why the Bible repeatedly calls them deceivers, liars, and corrupt-minded people. It is why Paul, Peter, and John reserve their most severe language and scathing indictments for false

> "Test the spirits to see whether they are from God."
> 1 John 4:1

teachers of the gospel. Like the Good Shepherd, we must continually warn people that false teachers "come to you in sheep's clothing but inwardly are ravenous wolves."

2. AVOID FALSE TEACHERS

Every believer must be alert to recognize false teachers and avoid them. Wolfgang had faithfully followed the example of Paul, who warned the Christians in Rome "to watch out" for false teachers and to "avoid them":

> I appeal to you, brothers, to *watch out for those who cause divisions* and create obstacles contrary to the doctrine that you

have been taught; *avoid them*. For such persons do not serve our Lord Christ, but their own appetites, and by smooth talk and flattery they deceive the hearts of the naïve. (Rom. 16:17-18; italics added)

In the words of biblical commentator, Robert Haldane, "No injunction ought to be attended to with more vigilance than this [avoid false teachers]."[4] In practical terms this means we are not to attend their Bible studies or go into their homes for fellowship and friendship. We are not to welcome them into our homes for hospitality (2 John 10-11). We must not give them a platform because once they are in a church they take hold like deep-rooted weeds that can't be easily removed. Whenever possible, we must avert conflict with false teachers by avoiding them.

In some cases, the false teachers themselves cannot be avoided, but their senseless debates can be avoided. The false teachers Timothy faced were argumentative and were caught up in worthless speculation. So Paul instructs Timothy to "have nothing to do with foolish, ignorant controversies" (2 Tim. 2:23). Paul wanted him to avoid being dragged into debates that would fuel conflict and controversy.[5] He did not want debates to give false doctrines and ideas undeserved credibility.

Paul, Peter, and John reserve their most stern language and scathing indictments for false teachers of the gospel.

On the positive side, instead of arguing with false teachers, Paul instructed his coworker Timothy to patiently and consistently "preach the word" (2 Tim. 4:1-2) and to be devoted "to the public reading of Scripture, to exhortation, to teaching" (1 Tim. 4:13).[6] By doing this, he would "save both" himself and his "hearers" (1 Tim. 4:16).

Although Wolfgang had warned the believers about the threat of false teachers, and specifically a popular movement in India called the Melchizedek movement, they failed to heed his warning. So when the itinerant missionaries arrived, the people were foolishly naïve. Seemingly unaware of the dangers, they did not turn away these agents of Satan.

---

[4]Robert Haldane, *Exposition of the Epistle to the Romans* (Edinburgh: Oliphant, 1874), 642.
[5]See also 1 Tim. 4:7; 6:20; 2 Tim. 2:16; Titus 3:9.
[6]See also 1 Tim. 4:6, 11, 16; 6:2; See also Titus 2:1, 7-8, 15.

They did not "test the spirits to see whether they [were] from God." Instead, they were curious to hear what they had to say and welcomed them to teach. This was a big mistake.

3. CONFRONT AND STOP FALSE TEACHERS

The new missionaries that came to the churches Wolfgang had established appeared to be extremely knowledgeable teachers of Scripture. But they were actually part of a movement that claimed to follow the apostle Thomas, the first missionary to India. Using the references to Melchizedek, an Old Testament priest to God, in the book of Hebrews,[7] they taught that Thomas established a special order of priests—the Melchizedek priests—to protect Jesus' teaching from corruption.

These teachers claimed that Wolfgang did not understand the full gospel message. They taught that complete salvation required separation from the world, the attainment of a certain degree of higher knowledge, and the practice of good works as prescribed by the Melchizedek Priesthood. These missionary teachers were self-confident and assertive. They boasted of their knowledge, rich heritage, and their founder, the apostle Thomas. They criticized Wolfgang's simple gospel message of salvation by grace alone, through faith alone, and in Christ alone. They also questioned Wolfgang's credentials and the churches in Germany that had sent him.

As a result, many of the people began to question Wolfgang's message and credibility. Fighting soon broke out in each of the churches. Some sided with the Melchizedek missionaries, some resisted, but most were confused as to who was right. Soon people were pitted against one another in angry debate. Accusations were flying in every direction. No one was safe from attack. It appeared that some of the churches would split apart.

When Wolfgang learned that the missionaries were infiltrating the churches, he wrote a lengthy letter to the churches refuting the missionaries' distorted doctrines. He carefully followed the example of Paul's reasoning and methods in his letters to the Galatians and Corinthians. He told his readers that he was shocked by how quickly

---

[7]Heb. 5:6; 6:20-7:25.

they had deserted the gospel for a different gospel and had allowed false teachers to deceive them. Using Paul's own words, he wrote:

> But I am afraid that as the serpent deceived Eve by his cunning, your thoughts will be led astray from a sincere and pure devotion to Christ. For if someone comes and proclaims another Jesus than the one we proclaimed, or if you receive a different spirit from the one you received, or if you accept a different gospel from the one you accepted, you put up with it readily enough. (2 Cor. 11:3-4)

Wolfgang reminded his dear friends of Jude's important exhortation to "contend for the faith." Heretics had infiltrated the church, so Jude exhorted every believer—not just church leaders—to identify the heretics and courageously strive for the preservation of the true faith. In the opening of his letter, Jude writes, "I found it necessary to write appealing to you to contend for the faith that was once for all delivered to the saints" (Jude 3).

Wolfgang also wrote a separate letter to the church leaders presenting many biblical passages that describe what false teachers are like and how church leaders are to deal with them. When the church leaders received the letter, they were truly amazed by all the information the Bible provided on the character of false teachers and how to deal with them. Wolfgang's letter pointed out three significant examples of how Paul, like a good shepherd, defended the gospel and his churches against the attack of wolves. He charged the church shepherds to follow these biblical examples in dealing with the invading itinerant missionaries.

a. Fighting Off Wolves in the New Church at Antioch

The first attack by false teachers recorded in the book of Acts was by Jewish Christian teachers from Jerusalem who came to the newly established church in Antioch. They taught that Gentile believers must be circumcised according to the custom of Moses in order to be saved. Paul and Barnabas immediately confronted this erroneous teaching. Luke writes that Paul and Barnabas "had no small dissension and debate with them" (Acts 15:2). These teachers could not be avoided. They had to be immediately confronted and stopped before their false gospel took hold in the minds of the people.

Soon after debating these Judaizing teachers in Antioch, Paul and Barnabas traveled to Jerusalem where the false teaching had originated. The twelve apostles, the elders of Jerusalem, and Paul and Barnabas convened to "debate" the issue. They concluded that salvation is "through the grace of the Lord Jesus" and "by faith" in his atoning death upon the cross, not by observance of the law (Acts 15:7-11). Because Barnabas and Paul took an uncompromising stand against the false teachers, a great victory was won for the gospel and a serious doctrinal conflict was resolved peacefully (Acts 15:4-29).

Note that if Paul, and the other apostles, had not struggled to defend the gospel against these first false teachers, we would have no gospel to preach today. One reason that so many seminaries and churches have lost "the word of truth, the gospel" is that too many church officials and trustees are afraid to confront and stop false teachers within their organizations. To make sure the gospel message is not lost in our own churches and institutions, we must courageously speak up and defend "the word of truth, the gospel of your salvation" (Eph. 1:13).

b. Fighting Off Wolves in the New Churches of Galatia

Itinerant Judaizing missionaries also infiltrated the new churches in Galatia. Paul wrote his impassioned letter to the Galatians in order to save his converts from the jaws of ferocious wolves. In this remarkable letter to the Galatian churches, we get a powerful example of how Paul reasoned from Scripture with his converts to correct their erroneous thinking. In this letter, Paul also informs his readers that when he was in Jerusalem, false Christians attempted to add the requirements of circumcision and Torah observance to the gospel message. He emphasizes his adamant refusal to compromise the gospel:

> We did *not yield in submission even for a moment*, so that the truth of the gospel might be preserved for you. (Gal. 2:5; italics added)

Refusing to yield for even a moment to false teachers and their pseudo-gospel must be the mindset of every faithful shepherd of God's flock. "Faithfulness" is a fruit of the Spirit (Gal. 5:22).

c. Correcting Friends and Fellow Apostles

Paul demonstrated tremendous courage and faithfulness to the gospel even when it required him to confront his fellow apostles and close friends. When Peter and Barnabas withdrew from their Gentile brothers and sisters in order to please certain legalistic teachers from Jerusalem, Paul charged them with misrepresenting the gospel and dividing the church:

> But when Cephas [Peter] came to Antioch, I opposed him to his face, because he stood condemned. For before certain men came from James, he was eating with the Gentiles; but when they came he drew back and separated himself, fearing the circumcision party. And the rest of the Jews acted hypocritically along with him, so that even Barnabas was led astray by their hypocrisy. But when I saw that their conduct was not in step with the truth of the gospel, I said to Cephas before them all . . . how can you force the Gentiles to live like Jews? (Gal. 2:11-14)

Although Paul's words may seem harsh and intolerant to us, they were motivated by his love for the gospel and the people of God. By caring enough to confront even his friends and coworkers, Paul was fulfilling his God-given task of defending the gospel and preserving "the unity of the Spirit in the bond of peace" (Eph. 4:3).

Wolfgang admonished the church leaders to act as Paul did and immediately take action to stop the itinerant missionaries from teaching their false gospel. He reminded them that this was exactly what Paul charged Timothy and Titus to do. When the church in Ephesus was in the death grip of false teachers, Paul ordered Timothy to immediately "charge certain persons not to teach any different doctrine" and thus save the church from the spread of lethal, unorthodox doctrines (1 Tim. 1:3). And in the letter to Titus, Paul orders Titus and the church elders on the island of Crete to "rebuke them sharply," that is, the false teachers, for "they must be silenced" (Titus 1:11, 13). To allow these disruptive, false teachers to continue to teach in the churches would be spiritual suicide.

"We did not yield in submission even for a moment, so that the truth of the gospel might be preserved for you." Galatians 2:5

———— ❧ ————

Wolfgang included in his letter to the church shepherds a lengthy quotation by the sixteenth-century reformer Martin Luther, to remind all church shepherds that they are required not only to feed the sheep, but to chase off wolves that would devour the sheep:

> A preacher must not only feed the sheep so as to instruct them how they are to be good Christians, but he must also keep the wolves from attacking the sheep and leading them astray with false doctrine and error; for the devil is never idle. Nowadays there are many people who are quite ready to tolerate our preaching of the Gospel as long as we do not cry out against the wolves and preach against the prelates.
>
> But though I preach the truth, feed the sheep well, and give them good instruction, this is still not enough unless the sheep are also guarded and protected so that the wolves do not come and carry them off.[8]

4. EXPEL FALSE TEACHERS FROM THE CHURCH

Wolfgang was discouraged when he heard that the churches he had planted were being torn apart by these itinerant teachers. Since his first letter, the church leaders had made an effort to stop the Melchizedek missionaries from teaching, but the missionary teachers would not listen. They only wanted to argue more. Furthermore, many of the believers were still fighting among themselves and the churches were growing increasingly divided over the claims of the itinerants. So in his second letter to the church leaders, Wolfgang knew he needed to

---

[8]Ewald M. Plass, ed., *What Luther Says: A Practical In-Home Anthology for the Active Christian* (St. Louis, MO: Concordia Publishing House, 1959), 1053 (entry 3351).

emphasize Titus 3:10-11 and tell the church leaders that the itinerant missionaries were a divisive group that needed to be warned and, if not responsive to biblical correction, expelled from the church:

> As for a person who stirs up division,[9] after warning him once and then twice, have nothing more to do with him, knowing that such a person is warped [corrupt] and sinful; he is self-condemned. (Titus 3:10-11)

The word "warning" (or "admonition") includes the idea of corrective instruction. Admonition seeks to change wrong behavior or belief with the goal of winning the offender.[10] One reason for the first and second admonition is that it is, as one scholar states, "a pastoral attempt to reclaim rather than a disciplinary measure, though there is a place for this if the corrective word is of no avail."[11] But if a divisive person persists, the third and final step is to "have nothing more to do with him."

Paul's precise meaning is debatable, but since the divisive person is rebellious, self-willed, and unwilling to submit to authority, it is reasonable to think that discipline entails putting the person out of church fellowship. The Greek word for "have nothing more to do with him" is best translated as "dismiss" or "expel."[12] Such divisive people (whether false teachers or not) are beyond reasoning with, for they love nothing more than to argue and fight. The only way to stop them and their divisive, sinful behavior is to expel them from the believing community.

Paul says that discipline against a divisive person must be carried out because "such a person is warped and sinful; he is self-condemned" (Titus 3:11). This statement of character shows the seriousness of the situation and the danger to the church body. A person who will not listen to warnings or receive corrective instruction will continue to divide the

[9]"A person who stirs up division," (*hairetikos*), refers to a divisive, factious person: "causing divisions, *factious, division-making*" (BDAG, 28).

[10]"Warning" (*nouthesia*) "counsel about avoidance or cessation of an improper course of conduct, *admonition, instruction*. . . . Of quiet reproof about repetition of an improper course of conduct *admonition, rebuke* Titus 3:10" (BDAG, 679).

[11]Johannes Behm, "*noutheteō, nouthesia*," in TDNT, 4 (1968): 1022.

[12]"Have nothing more to do with him," (*paraiteomai*), "here the word probably has the sense *discharge, dismiss, drive out*" (BDAG, 764).

flock if not stopped. Decisive, severe action is necessary because peace and unity will not be restored until the person is gone.

To reinforce the need to take strong, decisive action for protecting the church, Wolfgang reminded the church leaders that Paul handed over to Satan two of the leading false teachers who were destroying the church in Ephesus:

> Some have made shipwreck of their faith, among whom are Hymenaeus and Alexander, whom I have handed over to Satan that they may learn not to blaspheme. (1 Tim. 1:19-20; see also 1 Cor. 5:5)

These false teachers represented a fierce, spiritual battle between Satan and Christ, truth and lies, good and evil, light and darkness. Taking the toughest, strongest action possible, he expelled and handed over these false teachers to Satan, from whom they received their ideas (1 Tim. 4:1).

A person who will not listen to warnings or receive corrective instruction will continue to divide the flock if not stopped.

Please notice that even in this judgment, there was mercy. Paul disciplined these men so that they would be taught not to "blaspheme." "It is a consoling thought," writes one commentator, "that even such evil-doers are not irrecoverably beyond the reach of divine grace. The terrible sentence which befell them was, on the contrary, to teach by discipline those who refused to be taught by the truth."[13]

5. CORRECT WITH GENTLENESS AND FIRMNESS

As a wise student of people, Wolfgang feared that the churches' leaders would, because of their initial failure to protect the churches, overreact with anger and harshness. So at the end of his second letter to the church leaders, he reminded them to act according to biblical principles of conduct even when dealing with their opponents. When addressing false teachers and their

---

[13]William Kelly, *An Exposition of the Two Epistles to Timothy*, 3rd ed. (London: Hammond, 1948), 27.

followers, the goal is not to "bite and devour" but to teach and correct with the right attitude and in a distinctly Christian way (2 Tim. 2:24-26).

Because dealing with false teachers is terribly frustrating, there is a natural temptation to act in anger, impatience, or without concern for the soul of the opponent. But harsh, arrogant, or rude behavior wins no one. Such attitudes repel people and cause them to harden their hearts against God. So when we confront those who are in error—even if we must expel false teachers from the church—we are to demonstrate our Lord's character and display the fruit of the Spirit, not the works of the flesh.

In his instructions to Timothy, Paul describes what ought to be the demeanor of the Lord's servant when dealing with false teachers and their followers:

> The Lord's servant must not be quarrelsome but kind to everyone, able to teach, patiently enduring evil, correcting his opponents [false teachers] with gentleness. God may perhaps grant them repentance leading to a knowledge of the truth and they may escape from the snare of the devil, after being captured by him to do his will. (2 Tim. 2:24-26)

We must remember that we are not in a battle of wits against people in opposition to us; rather, we are in a battle against spiritual forces in opposition to God (Eph. 6:12-17). Thus the intent of our correction is that by God's mercy even false teachers will repent, "come to the knowledge of the truth," and "escape from the snare of the devil, having been captured by him to do his will." Therefore, we are not to adopt the methods and manners of false teachers, but are "to engage them with sound teaching and a godly demeanor."[14]

It is truly frightening to realize that some have been ensnared by the devil and held captive as his slaves. Only the Lord can deliver them, but we are his instruments of correction. By correcting opponents in a spirit of kindness, patience, gentleness, and with sound doctrinal teaching, there is a greater possibility that their hearts will be softened and won for the Lord.

One scholar accurately and succinctly summarizes the teaching

---

[14]Philip H. Towner, *The Letters to Timothy and Titus*, NICNT (Grand Rapids: Eerdmans, 2006), 794.

of the Pastoral Epistles on how the Lord's servant is to deal with false teachers:

> It is significant that the Pastoral Epistles, which more than any other New Testament writings insist on discipline in the form of admonition, prohibition and if necessary excommunication, also lay great stress on the fact that the true servant of the Lord will do all that can be done by way of love and patience that God may free those who go astray from the snares of Satan and bring them to repentance (2 Tim. 2:24-26).[15]

Some believers, Wolfgang acknowledged, were already in "the snare of the devil" and held "captive by him to do his will." Directing the church leaders' attention to Jude 22-23, Wolfgang urged them to show mercy and to seek to rescue those ensnared by the devil—but also to be careful to protect themselves from the cunning dangers of the false teachers. He pointed out that Jude's words were especially appropriate for dealing with their particular situation:

> And have mercy on those who doubt; save others by snatching them out of the fire; to others show mercy with fear, hating even the garment stained by the flesh. (Jude 22-23)

Wolfgang was a compassionate, merciful man, so it grieved him terribly to see people taken captive by the cunning lies of false teachers. He would do all in his power to rescue a person from "the snare of the devil." Since many of his converts were confused and deceived by the false teachers, he wanted the church leaders to show mercy to "those who doubt" and those in peril for their eternal souls.

Wolfgang's second letter to the church leaders moved them to take swift action. All of the leaders met together for a day of prayer, fasting, studying the Scriptures, and discussion of Wolfgang's letter. They realized that they had failed to protect their flocks from wolves and publicly confessed this failure to their churches.

The most gifted teachers and leaders among them confronted the false teachers. They did not argue with them, but told them in

---

[15]Joachim Jeremias, *"kleis,"* in TDNT, 3 (1965): 752, note 82.

no uncertain terms to stop teaching their erroneous doctrines. Some of the Melchizedek missionaries left, but others stayed and refused to stop their teaching and proselytizing. The church leaders instructed the people to have nothing more to do with the false teachers and publicly expelled them from their churches. Some church members left with the false teachers, but most stayed.

The believers had much work to do to repair the damage done to relationships because of the many angry words and cruel accusations made against one another. Most of them had acted in the flesh, not in the Spirit. To help restore sound doctrine and repair damaged relationships, the churches' leaders organized an intensive, five-day conference to teach the foundational principles of the gospel and Spirit-directed attitudes and behaviors for the believing community. They invited all Christians from their state in India to attend. Thousands came and were strengthened in their faith. Church leaders publicly committed themselves to teaching sound doctrine and becoming better equipped to shepherd and protect their flocks.

Wolfgang's letter concluded with two portions of Scripture to challenge and encourage the church leaders until his return to India:

> By the Holy Spirit who dwells within us, guard the good deposit [gospel] entrusted to you. (2 Tim. 1:14; also 1 Tim. 6:20)

> And now I commend you to God and to the word of his grace [the gospel], which is able to build you up and to give you the inheritance among all those who are sanctified. (Acts 20:32)

As for a person who stirs up division, after warning him once and then twice, have nothing more to do with him.
Titus 3:10

Principles to Remember

1. If possible, avoid false teachers and the conflict they create.

2. If false teachers of the gospel are in your church causing conflict, be faithful and courageous. Confront and stop them.

3. When dealing with false teachers and their followers, correct, rebuke, and teach in a spirit of gentleness, patience, and mercy.

10

Face Controversy

*And the Lord's servant must not be quarrelsome but kind to everyone, able
to teach, patiently enduring evil, correcting his opponents with gentleness.*
2 Timothy 2:24-25

Certain doctrines form the foundation for the whole structure of the
Christian faith. These doctrinal truths cannot be denied without the
structure crashing to the ground. False teachers of the gospel, as we
saw in chapter nine, create serious doctrinal controversy because they
undermine or deny these foundational truths.

However, there is also doctrinal controversy among evangelical,
Bible-believing Christians. Most of these controversies are not over
the essential, foundational truths of the gospel but are over what we
will call *important*, yet not *essential*, doctrines. Disagreements over
such doctrines do not indicate rejection of the gospel or the supreme
authority of Scripture, nor do they affect our eternal salvation.

Important doctrinal issues that often lead to controversy
include: Arminianism and Calvinism, Dispensationalism and Covenant
theology, premillennialism and amillennialism, creation and evolution,
men and women's roles in the church, baptism of the Holy Spirit and
spiritual gifts, modes of baptism, church polity, or issues of sanctification.
To further complicate matters, a good deal of controversy exists within
each of these doctrinal positions.

We must ask ourselves, *How are we to handle serious doctrinal
disagreements among our fellow believers who equally love God's Word and
all that is in it?* Even trying to address this age-old question is complicated
and will itself cause controversy. People have different temperaments and
handle controversy differently. Some are hot-tempered and can't deal
with doctrinal disputes without sparking heated, destructive debates.
Some are rigidly dogmatic while others are indifferent to doctrinal
disagreement. Some relish controversy. Others deal with doctrinal
disagreement with an objective mind and a gracious, understanding
spirit.

The individual believer's conscience also plays a role in addressing doctrinal differences. The conscience of some believers is so doctrinally sensitive that they cannot tolerate much disagreement in doctrine. They may limit their fellowship to a small circle of people with whom they agree. Other believers can tolerate a great deal of doctrinal diversity without violating their conscience. They may be able to work with others across doctrinal and denominational boundaries.

A person's religious heritage can be a significant factor in doctrinal controversy. Some believers have a rich church heritage that they love. They may have been trained from childhood in a certain denominational tradition and may react angrily to criticism of their beliefs. Other believers have no connection with a particular theological tradition or denomination and may view most denominational controversies as trivial and unimportant.

We must remember that doctrinal issues are often complex and entail multiple levels of issues (as is true in the debate over Arminianism and Calvinism). To further complicate matters, some doctrinal disagreements, such as different views of men and women's roles in the church and family, are more emotionally charged than others. So there are no simple answers to the problem of God's children fighting among themselves over important doctrines of the faith.

Although an entire book could be written on the subject of doctrinal differences, I will limit my remarks to the right behaviors and attitudes for handling conflict biblically and will focus on certain biblical truths that we should be able to agree upon for handling doctrinal controversy. To illustrate the problem and to set the tone for the rest of the chapter, let us consider the doctrinal conflict between George Whitefield and John Wesley, two of the greatest evangelists and men of God in the eighteenth century. God used both Whitefield and Wesley mightily to bring spiritual revival to England and to the colonies in America. Historians consider these spiritual revivals, particularly The Great Awakening in the American colonies, to be among the greatest known revivals in the past two thousand years of church history.

The two men started out as friends at Oxford. They worked as fellow evangelists until it became apparent that they were on opposing sides of the question of divine election: George Whitefield was a staunch Calvinist and John Wesley a passionate Arminian. Their disagreement over this important subject issued in much frustrating correspondence, sharp discussions, and a good deal of pulpit drama between the two. Both published and distributed sermons and papers defending their viewpoint. Each viewed the other as involved in serious doctrinal error with which there could be no compromise. Their differences stirred highly emotional debate among believers, and their friendship and Christian brotherhood was sorely tested.

Both men expressed their abhorrence that controversy had divided them and the spiritual revival that they had spawned. In a letter to Wesley, Whitefield confessed, "I cannot bear the thought of opposing you."[1] At another time he wrote, "May all disputing cease, and each of us talk of nothing but Jesus and him crucified."[2]

Although they tried, the two men never resolved their differences on divine election. In time, they did reconcile their relationship. Both men demonstrated publicly their enormous respect and sincere love for the other. They prayed regularly for each other, corresponded, and even tried to unite their divided revival movement.

At the end of his life, Whitefield requested that Wesley preach at his funeral, which he did. At Whitefield's funeral, Wesley commented, "How few have we known of so kind a temper, of such large and flowing affections . . . [Love] shone in his very countenance, and continually breathed in all his words."[3] Reflecting the same feeling of respect, Whitefield had previously written to Wesley, "The regard I have always had for you is still great, if not greater than ever; and I trust we shall give this and future ages an example of true Christian love abiding, notwithstanding differences in judgment."[4]

Wesley and Whitefield serve as relevant examples to us today. Regarding the theological tensions between these two legends of church history and our own issues of debate today, Iain Murray gives sound biblical counsel:

---

[1]John Pollock, *John Wesley* (Wheaton, IL: Victor, 1989), 141.
[2]Ibid., 150.
[3]Arnold Dallimore, *George Whitefield: The Life and Times of the Great Evangelist of the 18th Century Revival* (Carlisle, PA: Banner of Truth, 1980), 2: 511.
[4]Iain H. Murray, *Wesley and Men Who Followed* (Carlisle, PA: Banner of Truth, 2003), 71.

Doctrinal differences between believers should never lead to personal antagonism. Error must be opposed even when held by fellow members of Christ, but if that opposition cannot co-exist with a true love for all the saints and a longing for their spiritual prosperity then it does not glorify God nor promote the edification of the Church.[5]

An important lesson to be learned from Whitefield and Wesley is that godly Christians can be mightily used by the Holy Spirit, yet hold significantly different theologies on important doctrinal subjects. Furthermore, in the midst of our doctrinal differences, as many and as severe as they may be, we are to display godly principles of conduct and attitude. The following biblical truths serve as guidelines to help us keep controversy in right perspective when we face painful doctrinal disagreement with our beloved brothers and sisters in Christ.

1. WE ARE ACCOUNTABLE TO BIBLICAL AUTHORITY

Since, for Protestant Christians, no one person, denomination, or local church speaks for all believers and churches, we each are responsible to seek God's truth in his written revelation, the Holy Scriptures. Scripture is our supreme authority that judges our teachers, our traditions, and our churches. Our conscience is to be bound to God's Word.

All teachers, no matter how devout and scholarly, are fallible interpreters of God's Word. The greatest Christian teachers of the past two thousand years have been guilty of mixing error—in some cases, serious error—with truth. Let us not put any teacher, no matter how great or dearly beloved, on a pedestal of perfection. Instead, let us be like the first Berean Christians who heard Paul preach the gospel and *"received the word with all eagerness, examining the Scriptures daily to see if these things were so"* (Acts 17:11; italics added). The Bereans received teaching from the very mouth of Paul, the apostle, yet they still tested everything they heard by the authority of Scripture.

God desires that all his children know him through his Word

---

[5]Iain Murray, "Prefatory Note" in *George Whitefield's Journals* (Carlisle, PA: Banner of Truth, 1960), 568.

and faithfully obey his Word. When facing doctrinal controversy, we are not to be passive observers. We are to prayerfully seek the Holy Spirit's help to understand God's Word (1 John 2:20-21, 27); we are to work diligently to accurately interpret God's Word (2 Tim. 2:15); we are to consult other believers, past and present, who know and teach God's Word (Eph. 3:18). We are not to suspend our God-given ability to make critical judgments, to reason from Scripture, to discriminate truth from lies, or to pursue the truths that God has graciously given to us to know and enjoy. As Scripture itself says, "test the spirits to see whether they are from God" (1 John 4:1).[6]

Controversy over Bible doctrines should never stop us from the joy of searching, studying, and meditating on God's Word. With God's Word as our authority, we can rebuke erroneous teachings, change unbiblical traditions, sharpen people's thinking, and resolve differences (2 Tim. 3:16-17). When we are engaged in doctrinal controversy in the family of God, let's recognize that plenty of Scripture is plainly understandable and that God's children can know what is necessary to live an ethical, holy life that pleases their Lord. *Let us not forget that Scripture clearly reveals how we are to speak to and behave toward one another:* We are not to bite and devour one another.

2. THERE IS ONE GOSPEL

Despite our many differences, all believers agree on the essential, foundational truths that save our souls and give us new life. Christ, the sinless Lamb of God, died upon the cross for our sins and was raised from the dead (1 Cor. 15:3-4). By God's grace alone, not our human efforts, we are justified and reconciled to God through faith (Rom. 3:21-4:25). Jesus is Lord, and we presently await his glorious return when he will end all our controversies and sad divisions and bring perfect clarity to all biblical truth. Until that day, we will have to live and struggle with heart-breaking, doctrinal controversies and divisions.

If we understood all that the gospel entails, however, we would realize how much truth all believers share in common concerning the greatest questions and ultimate issues of life: Who is God? How did

---

[6]See also 1 Thess. 5:21; 1 Cor. 12:10; 14:29; Rev. 2:2.

the universe begin? What is the origin of evil and suffering? What is our authority for knowing truth? What are the fundamental moral and ethical principles for living a holy life? How do we know our sins are forgiven? Where will we spend eternity? Few secular people can agree on these fundamental life issues.

> "The best remedy then for divisions among Christians is for all to put first the living and teaching of the Gospel."
> —Iain Murray

So in the midst of doctrinal debates, many of which are worthy of our full effort and time, let us not lose focus on our God-given call to share the gospel with a lost world. Until Christ comes, we are to concern ourselves chiefly with the centrality of the gospel that saves and keeps us. We are, in our Lord's final words in Matthew's Gospel, to:

> make disciples of all nations, baptizing them in the name of the Father and of the Son and of the Holy Spirit, teaching them to observe all that I have commanded you. (Matt. 28:19-20)

In keeping with our Lord's teaching, Iain Murray helps to put our differences in balanced perspective:

> At the same time it is essential to recognize . . . that differences of understanding among Christians are never to be allowed to transcend the truth which makes them one in Christ. God would use our defective understandings and mistakes to humble us and to make us the more diligent in seeking to know the truth. The devil would use the same weakness to alienate believers from one another and to destroy Christian love and sympathy. . . . He would have issues not foundational to salvation so elevated in importance that the larger Christian unity disappears and contention threatens to 'destroy the work of God' (*Rom.* 14:20). This ploy Satan used with effect at the time of the Reformation and again in the Puritan period, for it is not Laodiceans [Rev. 3:14-22] but those with the strongest attachment to Scripture who are most likely to be tempted in this way. From the harm done by the dogmatism of controversies over secondary issues the devil then tempts

other Christians, who observe it, to abandon contending for the faith altogether.

The best remedy then for divisions among Christians is for all to put first the living and teaching of the gospel. . . . When Christ is put first, when making disciples of all nations is the first priority, division is far more likely to occur where it should occur, between believers and the world.[7]

It is instructive to observe that although George Whitefield and John Wesley disagreed on some very important theological issues, each one continued to preach the gospel of Christ crucified and as a result saw many thousands of people converted to Christ. Despite their intense struggles with each other over doctrine, neither man lost his focus on preaching the gospel to the lost. As a result, the Holy Spirit worked effectively through the preaching of the Word.

3. WE ARE ONE BODY

The New Testament presents a Church made up of one body, one worldwide brotherhood and sisterhood, one baptism, one fellowship, and one faith:

> There is one body and one Spirit—just as you were called to the one hope that belongs to your call—one Lord, one faith, one baptism, one God and Father of all, who is over all and through all and in all. (Eph. 4:3-6)

Paul's sevenfold use of the word "one" in this passage stresses the unity of all God's people. *That profound truth—the "one body and one Spirit"—always should be before us, guiding our church policies, doctrinal controversies, and relationships with all other born-again believers.* The truth of the "one body and one Spirit" should help to warn and to protect us from our innate propensity toward sinful, sectarian thinking and pride.

---

[7]Iain H. Murray, *Evangelicalism Divided: A Record of Crucial Change in the Years 1950-2000* (Carlisle, PA: Banner of Truth, 2000), 309-310.

All believers share the very same divine *life* given by the Spirit even though we do not share the same *understanding*, or *light*, on all biblical doctrines. Despite our many differences, *we are the one body of Christ, members one of another.* We are one family: sons and daughters of the same heavenly Father and brothers and sisters of the same elder brother, Jesus Christ. We all pray to the same God and Father and can worship Christ together. Thus we must not view one another as enemies but as beloved family members. Truly realizing the sadness of our many divisions and endless controversies should deeply humble and grieve us.

We must not forget that there is a vast difference between disagreeing with false teachers of the gospel (who are not true believers) and having theological disagreements with true believers in the family of God. We have no oneness or unity with those who do not possess the life of God and do not accept the gospel of Scripture. As Paul told the Corinthians, "What fellowship has light with darkness? What accord has Christ with Belial?" (2 Cor. 6:14-15). But *we are one* with our brothers and sisters in Christ, and we would do well to emulate Puritan theologian John Owen's passion for the oneness of God's people:

> I confess I would rather, much rather, spend all my time and
> days in making up and healing the breaches and schisms
> that are amongst Christians than one hour in justifying our
> divisions. . . . But who is sufficient for such an attempt? The
> closing of differences amongst Christians is like opening the
> book of Revelation—there is none able or worthy to do it,
> in heaven or in earth, but the Lamb: when He will put forth
> the greatness of His power for it, it shall be accomplished,
> and not before. In the meantime, a reconciliation amongst all
> Protestants is our duty. . . . When men have labored as much
> in the improvement of the principle of forbearance as they
> have done to subdue other men to their opinions, religion will
> have another appearance in the world.[8]

Scripture forbids "divisions" within the one body of Christ, so we must always be "eager to maintain the unity of the Spirit in the

---

[8] Cited by D. Martyn Lloyd-Jones in *The Puritans: Their Origins and Successors* (Carlisle, PA: Banner of Truth, 1987), 75-76.

bond of peace" (Eph. 4:3). *We are to strive to express our oneness with all true believers in as many practical ways as possible.* At the same time, we are to maintain the truths of Scripture and protect our churches from error. Maintaining the unity of the Spirit and the truths of Scripture is a difficult balancing act for everyone. The thought-provoking imagery of J. C. Ryle gives us a picture of how to strike the right balance: "Keep the walls of separation as low as possible, and shake hands over them as often as you can."[9]

George Whitefield resolved to maintain his Calvinistic doctrines without compromise (as did Wesley his doctrines), yet he worked tirelessly for harmony among all true believers. It grieved him to see many of his followers behave with bitter hostility toward those who disagreed with him. In a letter explaining how he could be kind to someone who differed from him doctrinally and had slighted him, Whitefield expressed his convictions on maintaining gracious harmony with all who love the Lord and at the same time maintaining his own doctrinal integrity:

> "Keep the walls of separation as low as possible, and shake hands over them as often as you can."
> —J. C. Ryle

> My heart does not reproach me for my kindness and friendship with those that differ from me. I think I have been led by the Word and Spirit of God into this part of my conduct. . . . I cannot renounce those precious truths [divine election] that I have felt the power of, and which are taught me not of man, but of God. At the same time I would love all that love Jesus, though they differ from me in some points.[10]

4. WE ARE TO DISPLAY CHRISTIAN ATTITUDES

It is often stated with disapproval that doctrine divides. The fact is, doctrine does divide. This is not just a Christian problem. Any

---

[9]J. C. Ryle, *Charges and Addresses* (1903; reprint, Edinburgh: Banner of Truth, 1978), 297.
[10]Dallimore, *George Whitefield*, 2: 76.

meaningful theological, philosophical, or political idea put forth to the public will often divide people into opposing camps. This is a reality of life that we cannot avoid.

Of course, doctrine also unites. Believers are united in our beliefs in Christ's incarnation, his sinless life upon earth, his miraculous works, his death, burial, resurrection, the proclamation of the gospel, his second coming, and our eternal dwelling with him in the new heaven and earth. These doctrines unite us, but the fact is other doctrines divide us. Often, the doctrines that divide us into hostile, warring factions are not about trivial matters, but are about important truths that God has revealed to his people.

We can't eliminate controversy over important biblical doctrines, but we can, by the Spirit's help, control how we dispute with one another. We can determine that our attitudes and behaviors will emulate "the wisdom from above," which is, "first pure, then peaceable, gentle, open to reason, full of mercy and good fruits, impartial and sincere" (James 3:17).[11]

a. Don't Act in the Flesh

No matter how impassioned our disagreements, Spirit-indwelt believers always are to reflect the fruit of the Spirit, not the sinful works of the flesh. Doctrinal controversy too often brings out the worst in people. It stirs up the worst evils of the flesh. Thus the Scripture warns us, "Do not be overcome by evil, but overcome evil with good" (Rom. 12:21).

When engaged in doctrinal controversy, we are to control our anger so that it does not distort our reasoning power, corrupt our attitudes, or lead us to judge others without mercy. We are to control our tongue from inflammatory rhetoric and untruthful statements so that we do not slander those who differ from us.

Disagreeing with a brother over a doctrinal matter is one thing, but pouring out vile, angry accusations, distorting another person's beliefs, demonizing a godly saint, and acting belligerently or childishly is another matter.

---

[11]See also Eph. 4:1-3, 32; Col. 3:12-14; Phil. 2:5; 1 Peter 3:8.

i. Pride

The awful display of religious pride that accompanies many doctrinal controversies ought to trouble us greatly. I literally have watched believers belittle others with whom they disagree and then walk away with their nose pointed up in the air—showing off their pride of knowledge and rightness of doctrine. This behavior illustrates the flesh in action, not the Spirit of God at work in their lives (Gal. 5:26). Religious, pharisaical pride is a totally unacceptable attitude for a follower of Christ. If only we were as concerned about our own sinful pride as we are about other people's errors, we would be much better Christians and we would handle disagreements more graciously.

Scripture plainly warns that doctrinal knowledge without love and humility only inflates the ego and is of no lasting benefit to building up God's people.[12] We must warn people continually about the subtle sins and deceptions of religious pride.

ii. Quarrelsomeness

Although we are enjoined "to contend for the faith," we are not to be contentious people (Jude 3). Paul makes a distinction between the act of contending for the faith, which we are all to do, and having a quarrelsome spirit. In his letter to the Romans, Paul identifies a quarrelsome spirit as one of the works of the flesh and puts it on par with sins like "drunkenness" and "sexual immorality" (Rom. 13:13). Paul also chastens the Corinthians for being quarrelsome and "contentious"[13] and tells the Philippians to "do all things" without complaining and arguing (Phil. 2:14). He contrasts false teachers who have "an unhealthy craving for controversy and for quarrels about words" with the "Lord's servant" who "must not be quarrelsome" (2 Tim. 2:24).

Some believing Christians are so argumentative and combative that I think they would argue with Jesus Christ if he were here! Such people cause continual unrest in a church. Quarrelsome, argumentative people do not build up a church or generate peace. They are not peacemakers; they are troublemakers. For these reasons, a "quarrelsome" person does not meet the biblical qualifications to be a pastor elder (1 Tim. 3:3).

---

[12] 1 Cor. 8:1-3; 13:1-3.
[13] 1 Cor. 1:11; 11:16.

iii. Factions

Frustrated with the Corinthians' "divisions" within the church (1 Cor. 11:18), Paul makes the thought-provoking statement that "there must be factions among you in order that those who are genuine among you be recognized" (1 Cor. 11:19). Divisions and factions are sinful works of the flesh (Gal. 5:20) and denounced by Scripture (1 Cor. 1:10). Yet, there is a sense in which "there must be factions" in order to reveal the true character of the people of the church. God uses fighting and divisions for his own purpose to test and sift the congregation to reveal who are the genuine, faithful servants approved by the Lord. Factions separate the gold from the dross. Our behavior exposes our inner character and spiritual reality.

b. Act in the Spirit

Although 2 Timothy 2:24-26 addresses handling of false teachers and their followers, it also provides guidance for having the right attitudes toward our fellow believers with whom we disagree:

> And the Lord's servant must not be quarrelsome but kind to
> everyone, able to teach, patiently enduring evil, correcting
> his opponents with gentleness. God may perhaps grant them
> repentance leading to a knowledge of the truth, and they may
> escape from the snare of the devil, after being captured by him
> to do his will. (2 Tim. 2:24-26)

If Paul instructs us to be gentle, patient, and kind in our dealings with false teachers and their followers, how much more do we need to be gentle, patient, and kind with our brothers and sisters in Christ with whom we disagree over doctrine?

If only we would spend as much time studying and obeying what the Scripture teaches about Spirit-led speech, conduct, and attitudes as we spend studying the doctrines over which we fight, our churches would experience far fewer divisions and more profitable theological discussions. We must defend orthodox doctrine with orthodox behavior and speech. Alexander Ross comments:

But we must remember that the truth of Christianity cannot be advanced, or defended worthily, except in a Christian spirit, a fact which keen controversialists have not always remembered. Some ardent Christians may defeat their own ends by doubtful methods; the soundest theology may fail to appeal to the minds of outsiders, if it be advocated by men who are self-seeking partisans or men who are unscrupulous in their controversial activities.[14]

c. Don't Be Naïve

Some of our doctrinal differences are understandable and respectable, but others are not acceptable. During the past forty years, among Bible-believing Christians, there has been an explosion of aberrant doctrines— everything from promising a four-fold return on "seed money" to twisting Scripture to legitimize same-sex marriage.

We cannot be naïvely tolerant of these erroneous teachings. Pastoral care for God's people demands that false teachings be exposed and kept out of the local church. Christians can be terribly deceived about their beliefs. It is a shepherd's God-given duty to protect the flock from harm. A true shepherd will seek to expose deception and cast the light of truth on error. Paul's tough and tender dealings with the Corinthians is an outstanding example of how a good shepherd warns, rebukes, and patiently instructs those in his wayward flock who are deceived about their beliefs. His profound love for the Corinthians moved him to speak out against their wrong beliefs and behaviors. Sometimes we, too, will have to cry out, as Paul did: "Do not be deceived: 'Bad company ruins good morals.' Wake up from your drunken stupor" (1 Cor. 15:33-34).

Our differences regarding some doctrinal beliefs may be so significant with certain believers that they prevent us from ministering together. But, as brothers and sisters in the Lord, we can still pray together and enjoy each other's company on a personal level. At such times, we put our differences aside and focus on our Christian fellowship together and common beliefs in Christ. As Whitefield said to Wesley,

---

[14]Alexander Ross, *The Epistles of James and John*, NICNT (Grand Rapids: Eerdmans, 1954), 68.

"May all disputing cease, and each of us talk of nothing but Jesus and him crucified."[15]

5. LOVE GOD AND NEIGHBOR FOREMOST

The Bible's two greatest commandments are to love God and to love our neighbor:

> You shall love the Lord your God with all your heart and with all your soul and with all your mind. This is the great and first commandment. And a second is like it: You shall love your neighbor as yourself. On these two commandments depend all the Law and the Prophets. (Matt. 22:37-40)

We may have a "perfect" systematic theology, but if we don't love the Lord our God with all our hearts and love our neighbor with whom we disagree, our doctrine and practice remain defective.

We must defend orthodox doctrine with orthodox behavior and speech.

There is debate whether or not we will be quizzed at the judgment seat of Christ as to why we were premillennial or amillennial. But there is no doubt that we will be judged as to our love for God and neighbor. In the words of our Lord himself: "On these two commandments depend all the Law and the Prophets" (Matt. 22:40). "There is no other commandment greater than these" (Mark 12:31).

None of us has all doctrine straight, but every one of us can love God and neighbor despite our doctrinal shortcomings. Those with whom we disagree are often precious Christians who love the Lord, evangelize, worship Christ, and are passionate about global missions and mercy ministries. *We should be able to recognize and acknowledge their love for Christ and their loving sacrificial service to others.* We may even have to admit that they demonstrate a greater love for God and neighbor than we do.

Although Whitefield disagreed with Wesley strongly, he freely admitted Wesley's love for God and the lost. The story is told that "a

---

[15]Pollock, *John Wesley*, 150.

censorious professor of religion asked [Whitefield] 'whether he thought they would see John Wesley in heaven?' 'No, sir,' was the striking answer; 'I fear not. He will be so near the throne, and we shall be at such a distance, that we shall hardly get a sight of him.'"[16]

We should all passionately pursue loving God and neighbor more and always be encouraging one another to keep our priorities fixed on love for God and neighbor. On this point we can all heartily agree.

On the final night before his crucifixion, our Lord gave the disciples a new commandment: *Love one another just as I have loved you* (John 13:34-35). In keeping with our Lord's teaching, Peter declared, "Above all, keep loving one another earnestly, since love covers a multitude of sins" (1 Peter 4:8). In bold contrast to false teachers who use cunning deception in speech, believers are to speak "the truth in love," which helps the church grow in Christlike character (Eph. 4:14-15). Paul reminded the fighting Corinthians that love "is not arrogant," it does not "boast" of self; love, and only love, bears, believes, hopes, endures all things (1 Cor. 13:4, 7). He concluded his letter to them by saying, "Let all that you do be done in love" (1 Cor. 16:14). The statement, "all that you do," certainly applies to how we handle doctrinal controversy! Christlike love for one another in the one body of Christ is the key to handling our many frustrating controversies and warlike divisions.

One of the wonderful qualities of Christlike love is that it understands how fearful and difficult it is when our cherished, long-held beliefs are attacked or denied. Love understands that for some believers doctrinal disagreement is emotionally traumatizing, while for others the intellectual interaction of doctrinal debate is mentally stimulating.

Love seeks to understand and protect the beloved, not just win the argument or crush the opponent. So when we contend with one another over doctrinal matters, we would do well to keep in mind the Golden Rule of love: "So whatever you wish that others would do to you, do also to them, for this is the Law and the Prophets" (Matt. 7:12).

If we want others to represent our beliefs accurately, then we must do the same for our opponents.

---

[16]J. C. Ryle, *Christian Leaders of the Eighteenth Century* (1885; reprint, Carlisle, PA: Banner of Truth, 1978), 60.

If we want to be treated with respect, then we must respect those with whom we differ.

If we want to be treated with grace and understanding, then we must treat those who oppose us with grace and understanding.

If we want people to see what is good and right in what we do and believe, then we must acknowledge what is good in others.

"We shall give this and future ages an example of true Christian love abiding, notwithstanding differences in judgment."
—George Whitefield

If we want others to learn from our trusted Bible teachers and to read our printed material, then we should be willing to listen to their teachers and read their books (1 Cor. 3:21-23).

John Wesley and George Whitefield could not agree on certain important doctrines. Although they at times ministered together, their cooperation in the gospel ministry was limited in some respects. More important, they tried by the grace of God to act toward one another as principled men of God. They submitted their minds and conduct to the commands of Scripture. In this they are an example to us all. Whitefield had written to Wesley that he hoped that "we shall give this and future ages an example of true Christian love abiding, notwithstanding differences in judgment."[17] In this they largely succeeded. May we, as followers of Jesus Christ, by his grace and in the power of his Spirit, seek to live as such examples of Christian love.

Live in harmony with one another. . . . Never be conceited.
Romans 12:16

---

[17]Iain Murray, *Wesley and Men Who Followed*, 71.

Principles to Remember

1. When facing doctrinal conflict, remember that Bible-believing Christians all agree on the essential, foundational truths that save our souls and give us new life.

2. Let us never lose focus on our God-given call to share the gospel with a lost world.

3. We can't eliminate doctrinal controversy, but we can control our attitudes and behaviors. *Let all that we do* be done in love.

Appendix

Understanding the Word *Flesh*

Flesh (Greek, *sarx*) is literally the soft tissue part of the body. Like the grass and flowers of the field, flesh is perishable, transitory, fragile, and short-lived (1 Peter 1:24-25). Throughout Scripture, the word *flesh* is used in various ways, referring to the physical body as a whole, to an individual person, to the entire human race, to ethnic Israel or to one's lineage.

1. THE PASSIONS AND WORKS OF THE FLESH

In a number of passages in Galatians,[1] the term *flesh* is used negatively to describe the fallen human condition apart from the life of God. Some scholars refer to this negative use of the word *flesh* as the ethical or technical, theological use. The flesh is related to "the present evil age" from which Christ has delivered his people (Gal. 1:4). It represents the old, earthly, temporal order that is subject to the power of sin—weak, corruptible, and doomed to destruction. The flesh cannot be reformed or made acceptable to God by any religious practice. In stark contrast, "the Spirit" is of God and represents the new eternal order. Only the Spirit can give life and victory over the flesh.

Galatians 5 reveals that the flesh revolts against the Spirit and acts independently of the Spirit in a Christian's life. It has sinful "passions and desires"[2] that are opposed to the Spirit's desires:

> For the *desires* of the flesh are against the Spirit, and the *desires* of the Spirit are against the flesh, for these are *opposed to each other*, to keep you from doing the things you want to do. (Gal. 5:17; italics added)

---

[1] Gal. 5:13, 16-17, 19-21, 24; 6:8.
[2] Gal. 5:24; see also Gal. 5:16-17; Rom. 13:14; Eph. 2:3; 1 Peter 2:11; 1 John 2:16.

Furthermore, Galatians 5:19 asserts that "the works" that issue from the flesh should be clearly evident to God's people when they are displayed in our behavior or that of others. The "works of the flesh" cover every kind of conceivable sin: sexual lust, greed, laziness, selfish ambition, drunkenness, idolatry, jealousy, community strife, divisions, and conceit (Gal. 5:19-21, 26).

The flesh is preoccupied with its own self-interests and self-fulfillment (Gal. 5:13). It stands in bold contrast to love and humble servanthood (Gal. 5:14) and causes destruction of the believing community (Gal. 5:15, 26). Paul solemnly warns his readers that those who continually practice the works of the flesh will not inherit the kingdom of God (Gal. 5:21; 6:8).

2. TWO REALMS OF EXISTENCE

According to the New Testament, there are two contrasting realms of existence. People are either "in Adam" or "in Christ."[3] There is "the old self" or the "new self."[4] There is life "in the flesh" or life "in the Spirit."[5] To be identified with Adam and his race is to be in bondage to sin, death, and the flesh. To be identified with Christ and his new race (Eph. 2:15) is to have new life and to be set free from the bondage of sin and the flesh.

Before conversion to Christ, all believers "were living in the flesh" (Rom. 7:5) and, like all unregenerate people, "lived in the passions of the flesh, carrying out the desires of the [flesh]" (Eph. 2:3). We were "dead" in our "trespasses" and the "uncircumcision of [our] flesh" (Col. 2:13). Paul reveals the awful condition of those who live in the flesh and walk according to it:

> For those who live according to the flesh set their minds on the things of the flesh. . . . To set the mind on the flesh is death. . . . For the mind that is set on the flesh is hostile to God, for it does not submit to God's law; indeed, it cannot.

---

[3]Rom. 5:12-21; 1 Cor. 15:21-22; 15:45-49.
[4]Eph. 4:21-24; Col. 3:9-10; Rom. 6:6.
[5]Rom. 8:4, 7-13.

Those who are in the flesh cannot please God (Rom. 8:6-8). Then Paul points out a remarkable truth:

> You, however, are not in the flesh but in the Spirit, if in fact the Spirit of God dwells in you. . . . So then, brothers, we are debtors, not to the flesh, to live according to the flesh. (Rom. 8:9, 12)

Believers are "not in the flesh but in the Spirit!" At the point of conversion, a believer dies to the old realm of enslavement to the flesh and begins living in the new realm of the Spirit. Therefore, believers "walk not according to the flesh but according to the Spirit" (Rom. 8:4).

As believers, we have stripped off "the body of the flesh" at conversion through our union with Christ in his death (Col. 2:11). We are no longer under the bondage and domination of the flesh. Instead, we are "in the Spirit," and become "a new creation" in Christ (Gal. 6:15; 2 Cor. 5:17), which ushers us into a new realm of existence of eternal life and peace (Rom. 8:6) that is "free . . . from the law of sin and death" (Rom. 8:2). This new quality of life seeks to please and serve God and to live righteously according to God's Word. It produces Christlike behaviors and attitudes (Gal. 5:22-23).

3. STRUGGLING WITH THE FLESH

Unlike the non-Christian who lives life by the "passions and desires" of the flesh, all believers make a decisive, life-changing break with the flesh at the time of conversion. Believers have "crucified the flesh with its passions and desires" (Gal. 5:24) and now "live by the Spirit" who has given new life and power over sin and the flesh (Gal. 5:25; also Rom. 8:2).

Although "the flesh" and "the old self" have been crucified, it is painfully obvious that believers still sin. We are not exempt from the temptation of fleshly desires or from sinning (cf. Rom. 6:12; 8:13; Gal. 5:16-17). The reason for this seeming contradiction is that believers have yet to be fully delivered from this world of sin and death. *The power and bondage of sin has been broken, and believers have the Spirit, but the body has not yet been redeemed, so sin and the flesh still threaten and tempt believers.* Only at death or the final consummation will we experience full freedom—redemption from sin, the flesh, and the unredeemed body (Rom. 8:23):

> Since the resurrection is still impending, believers are not liberated in every respect from the present evil age (cf. 1 Cor. 15:20-28). They will still experience death, which is the consequence of the sin introduced by the first Adam. But they are guaranteed victory over death because they are incorporated into the second Adam. So too, believers will not experience perfect deliverance from sin in this age, so that they never sin at all. What has been shattered is not the *presence* of sin but the *mastery* of sin over believers. Paul uses a number of expressions to show that he is speaking of sin's dominion being broken instead of perfect sinlessness.[6]

In this struggle between "the desires of the flesh" and "the desires of the Spirit," believers cannot be neutral. The New Testament writers thus warn their readers against acting in the flesh as they did before their conversion. Paul warns the Galatians not to allow their new freedom in Christ to become "an opportunity for the flesh" (Gal. 5:13). To his readers in Rome, Paul says, "we are debtors, not to the flesh, to live according to the flesh" and "make no provision for the flesh, to gratify its desires" (Rom. 8:12; 13:14). Peter writes: "Beloved, I urge you as sojourners and exiles to abstain from the passions of the flesh, which wage war against your soul" (1 Peter 2:11).

Galatians 5 teaches that there is victory over the flesh by means of the presence of the Holy Spirit and by actively walking in step with the Spirit's leading (Gal. 5:16, 18, 25; 6:8). Thomas Schreiner's comments on this point bear repeating:

> A conflict between the flesh and the Spirit has ensued, explaining why it is so vital for believers to walk in and to be led by the Spirit. Therefore, walking in the Spirit is not the same thing as coasting along in a fair breeze, for the flesh wars

---

[6]Thomas R. Schreiner, *Romans*, BECNT (Grand Rapids: Baker, 1998), 317.

against the Spirit and the Spirit wars against the flesh. Still, Paul is fundamentally optimistic here, claiming that as one walks by the Spirit and is led by the Spirit, there is substantial, significant, and observable victory over the flesh.[7]

4. DEAD TO SIN AND ALIVE TO GOD

Similar to the way that Galatians speaks of believers as crucifying the flesh and living by the Spirit, Romans speaks of believers dying to sin through their union (Rom. 6:4-5) with Christ in his death, burial, and resurrection: "Our old self was crucified with him in order that the body of sin might be brought to nothing, so that we would no longer be enslaved to sin" (Rom. 6:6).

Before conversion, all believers were "slaves to sin" (Rom. 6:17, 20). But through our union with Christ, we have "died to sin" (Rom. 6:2) and have been "set free from sin" (Rom. 6:7, 18, 22). *As a result of Christ's death and resurrection and the coming of the Holy Spirit, the reign and rule of sin has been ended in a believer's life.*[8] As one Bible expositor succinctly put it, "sin remains, but does not reign in the Christian's life."[9] Consequently, Paul directs all believers to "Consider yourselves dead to sin and alive to God in Christ Jesus" (Rom. 6:11).

Because we are dead to sin and alive to God, Paul can also say, "Let not sin therefore reign in your mortal bodies, to make you obey their passions" (Rom. 6:12). Paul would not be able to say this to an unregenerate person. The unregenerate person is in the flesh and a slave to sin's reign and rule. The unregenerate person needs, in the words of Jesus, to be "born again" and "born of the Spirit" (John 3:3-8), and to pass "from death to life" (John 5:24). But believers are no longer helpless slaves of sin. Our identification with Christ's death, burial, and resurrection (Rom. 6:3-4) means that we have been raised to "walk in newness of life" (Rom. 6:4).

---

[7]Thomas R. Schreiner, *Galatians*, ZECNT (Grand Rapids: Zondervan, 2010), 345.

[8]Rom. 6:2, 7, 11, 14, 18, 22.

[9]Ben Witherington, III, *Grace in Galatia: A Commentary on St Paul's Letter to the Galatians* (Grand Rapids: Eerdmans, 1998), 378.

Thus the New Testament imperative for every believer is that we "walk by the Spirit," that is, live the Christian life by the Spirit's enabling power and leading (Gal. 5:16, 18, 25; 6:8). For believers, the empowering presence of the Holy Spirit is our means for resisting sin and the flesh. When we "walk by the Spirit," we will "not gratify the desires of the flesh" (Gal. 5:16). This is a promise of victory over the flesh. Walking by the Spirit is the biblical antidote to the problem of the flesh.

Allow me to illustrate how this works with a story about five college students who shared an apartment together. One was a believer, but the other four were not. The four unbelievers couldn't talk without using profane language and looked forward to weekends when they drank themselves silly and hooked up with girls at parties. They lived to fulfill the passions and desires of the flesh.

After a year of living together, the Christian student led his four fellow students to Christ. Immediately, there was a change of attitude and behavior in the four new believers. Without their roommate saying anything, each of the young men stopped swearing. They no longer looked forward to drunken parties and realized that they could no longer treat women like sex objects to satisfy their selfish pleasures. Instead, they started going to Bible studies, fellowshipping with other Christians, and began looking for Christian wives. They immediately found they possessed a new power over sin and the flesh, as well as new interests and aims in life. They no longer lived to indulge "the passions of our flesh" (Eph. 2:3).

Those young men still sin—they get angry and lust after women—but there is by the Spirit a new conviction in their minds about sin. Their conscience is sensitive and seeks to recognize their disobedience to God's Word. When they sin, they confess it and seek to behave in a way that pleases their new Lord and Master. This is what being born of the Spirit looks like in the lives of people who trust in Christ for salvation and have "crucified the flesh with its passions and desires" (Gal. 5:24).

5. PRACTICAL STEPS TO VICTORY

Since believers will struggle with sin and the flesh, Scripture gives practical instruction for gaining victory:

- We are to understand our new identity "in Christ," believe what God says in his Word about our new life in the Spirit, and act accordingly. "So you also must consider yourselves dead to sin and alive to God in Christ Jesus" (Rom. 6:11; also 8:2). "For sin will have no dominion over you, since you are not under law but under grace" (Rom. 6:14).

- We are to actively, day-by-day, moment-by-moment walk by the Spirit (Gal. 5:16), keep in step with the Spirit's leading (Gal. 5:18, 25), and "sow to the Spirit" (Gal. 6:8).

- We are not to allow our new freedoms in Christ to give the flesh an opportunity to seize what is good and tempt us into selfish displays of the flesh (Gal. 5:13).

- We are, by the Spirit's enablement, "to abstain from the passions of the flesh, which wage war against [our] soul[s]" (1 Peter 2:11).

- We are to "make no provision for the flesh, to gratify its desires" (Rom. 13:14).

- We are, "by the Spirit," to "put to death the deeds of the body" (Rom. 8:13; also Col. 3:5). The flesh cannot be reformed by any kind of religious practice. It has no eternal future. It must be put to death.

- We are to present ourselves "to God as those who have been brought from death to life," and our bodily members "to God as instruments for righteousness" (Rom. 6:13; also 6:19). We are to "present [our] bodies as a living sacrifice" (Rom. 12:1).

- We are not to present our bodily members "to sin as instruments for unrighteousness" (Rom. 6:13). We are not to be "conformed to this world" (Rom. 12:2).

When seeking to understand how to "walk by the Spirit," believers often ask for an explanation of the relationship between our personal responsibility and the Holy Spirit's active work in us to lead us to do God's will. To answer this relevant question, I cannot improve on the comments of Richard Longenecker and Graham Cole:

> ...for Paul never views the ethical activity of the believer apart from the Spirit's work nor the Spirit's ethical direction and enablement apart from the believer's active expression of his or her faith.[10]

> This process is concursive, which is to say that more than one agent is involved. God is at work and so too is the believer, as Philippians 2:12-13 shows. . . . How the Spirit effects these changes positively and negatively is not revealed. Mystery remains. Scripture is non-postulational. It does not offer theories concerning the nature of realities or processes. Instead it affirms that certain realities are so, and the believer by faith lives as if they are so, and in so doing finds that they indeed are so (*solvitur ambulando*, Lat., "It is solved by walking").[11]

---

[10]Richard N. Longenecker, *Galatians*, WBC (Dallas, TX: Word, 1990), 266.
[11]Graham A. Cole, *He Who Gives Life: The Doctrine of the Holy Spirit* (Wheaton, IL: Crossway, 2007), 229.

Index of Persons

Index of Scripture Citations

166

172

About the Author

For the past forty years Alexander Strauch has served as a teaching elder at the Littleton Bible Chapel in Littleton, Colorado. Additionally, he has taught philosophy and New Testament literature at Colorado Christian University. A gifted Bible teacher and popular speaker, Alexander Strauch has helped thousands of churches worldwide through his expository writing and preaching ministry. He is the author of more than a dozen books, including *Biblical Eldership* which has sold over 250,000 copies. Alexander Strauch's books have been translated into more than twenty languages.

Alexander and his wife Marilyn reside in Littleton, Colorado, near their four adult daughters and ten grandchildren.

For more details about Alexander Strauch and his books and audio messages, contact Lewis and Roth Publishers at 800-477-3239 or www.lewisandroth.org. If you are calling from outside the United States, please call 719-494-1800.

Acknowledgments

Christian friends are a wonderful gift from God's good hand. I am exceedingly blessed to have many skilled friends assist me in the completion of this book.

I am indebted especially to Paul and Laura Lundgren for their assistance and many helpful suggestions, Ryan Gold for checking sources, verifying quotations, and documenting footnotes, Dr. David MacLeod, who carefully checked the footnotes, and the encouragement of Reed Taussig and Doug VanSchooneveld. Special thanks to the editorial team of Amanda Sorenson, Shannon Wingrove, and Allan Sholes. They are a joy to work with, and their creative recommendations are greatly appreciated.

A great deal of gratitude is extended to Jay Brady, at Lewis & Roth Publishers, who helped me at every phase of the production of this book. He is a truly multitalented person. Also, I would like to thank Barbara Peek, who proofread the final manuscript.

I gratefully acknowledge the competent assistance of my secretary, Chelsea Van Ryn. Without her help I would still be in the process of writing this book.

As always, my deepest appreciation goes to Marilyn, my loving wife and chief partner in life and in service for the Lord.

Recommended Reading to Complement
If You Bite & Devour One Another

"The church in Ephesus was sound in doctrine and faithful to the gospel, but something was missing. The spirit of the church was defective. It lacked love. So let us explore Christ's remedy... so we can guard against such a failure in our own churches."
— *Alexander Strauch in* Love or Die

Love or Die: Christ's Wake-up Call to the Church
by Alexander Strauch

In his challenging exposition of Revelation 2:2-6, Strauch examines this alarming rebuke of Jesus Christ to his church. Part I of *Love or Die* reminds us that "an individual or a church can teach sound doctrine, be faithful to the gospel, be morally upright and hard-working, and yet be lacking love and therefore, be displeasing to Christ." Love can grow cold while outward religious performance appears acceptable--even praiseworthy.

Part Two of *Love or Die* presents practical ways to cultivate love in the local church, including chapters that challenge us to Study Love, Pray for Love, Teach Love, Model Love, Guard Love and Practice Love.

A five-lesson study guide is included, making this an exceptional tool for classes and small groups.

"Jesus commanded us to love God with all our heart, soul, and mind, and to love our neighbor as ourselves. Yet few Christians take those commands seriously. Alexander Strauch does, and in *Love or Die: Christ's Wake-up Call to the Church*, he helps us understand how to apply Jesus' commands both as individuals, and corporately in our churches. All believers will benefit from a serious study of this book."

— *Jerry Bridges, Author,* Pursuit of Holiness

"I can think of few books I've read recently that have had so immediate an impact on me and have given me so much to think about. I trust, that with God's help, the implications of this book will be with me always."
— *Tim Challies, Book Reviewer, discerningreader.com, Author,* The Discipline of Spiritual Discernment

Lewis & Roth Publishers
800.477.3239 ✦ **www.lewisandroth.org**

Recommended Reading to Complement
If You Bite & Devour One Another

*"The more difficult and potentially explosive the controversy among
true believers, the greater the need to display
more love, not less."*
— Alexander Strauch in Leading with Love

A Christian Leader's Guide to Leading with Love
by Alexander Strauch

Though a wealth of good material is available on the leadership qualities of courage, charisma, discipline, vision, and decisiveness, few books for church leaders include anything about love. This is a major oversight since the New Testament is clear that love is indispensable to service. In the absence of love, Christian leadership counts for nothing (1 Corinthians 13:1-3).

In *Leading with Love*, Strauch powerfully portrays love as the one leadership quality no church leader can afford to do without. "When leaders and teachers discover what the Bible says about love," he writes, "it dramatically improves their relationship skills, effectiveness in ministry, and ability to resolve conflict and division. Leading with love is indispensable to producing spiritually healthy churches, reaching others for Christ, and pleasing God. It all hinges on love."

If you lead or teach people--whether as a Sunday School teacher, youth worker, women's or men's ministry leader, Bible study leader, administrator, music director, elder, deacon, pastor, missionary or evangelist--this book will help you become a more loving leader or teacher. A study guide is also available.

"This message is urgently needed by all of us. You may have many talents and spiritual gifts, but without the love that this book speaks about, you don't really have much at all."
— *George Verwer, Founder, Operation Mobilization*

"An excellent meditation on 1 Corinthians 13 and Christian leadership."
— *Thabiti Anyabwile, Senior Pastor, First Baptist Church of Grand Cayman*

"*Leading with Love* demonstrates that love is indispensable for effective spiritual leadership. I hope this insightful study will receive the enthusiastic response it deserves and that it will be widely read."
— *Vernon Grounds, late Chancellor, Denver Seminary*

Lewis & Roth Publishers
800.477.3239 ♦ www.lewisandroth.org

Recommended Reading to Complement
If You Bite & Devour One Another

"To reform the Church of God we should always begin with self-re-
form. Schisms and divisions will increase so long as we begin with
reforming others."
— *R.C. Chapman as quoted in* Agape Leadership

Agape Leadership: Lessons in Spiritual Leadership from the Life of R.C. Chapman
by Alexander Strauch & Robert L. Peterson

Agape Leadership promises to be one of the most spiritually inspiring books you have ever read. Although little known today, R.C. Chapman was a widely respected Christian leader in England during the nineteenth century. Chapman became legendary in his own time for his gracious ways, his patience, his kindness, his balanced judgment, his ability to reconcile people in conflict, his absolute fidelity to Scripture, and his loving pastoral care. By the end of his life, Chapman was known worldwide for his love, wisdom and compassion.

"I recommend *Agape Leadership* as a useful resource, but it is only an appetizer for Peterson's longer work on Chapman's life, *Apostle of Love*. These two books...and Alexander Strauch's dynamic duo *Love or Die* and *Leading With Love*, will remind the Christian that Christ is the cornerstone of the Church, and that above all, Christ is love."

— *Mark Tubbs, Book Reviewer, discerningreader.com*

Robert Chapman: A Biography (Apostle of Love)
by Robert L. Peterson

Although he is not widely known today, Robert Chapman was one of the most respected Christians of his generation. His caring and humble attitude had a marked impact on the lives of such men as George Muller, J. Hudson Taylor, John Nelson Darby, and Charles Spurgeon. These notable men agreed that Chapman was a giant among them. This remarkable man served God in the small town of Barnstaple, England, during the nineteenth century.

Robert Chapman's life cannot help but challenge the Lord's people to deepen their devotion to Christ and love others more selflessly.

Lewis & Roth Publishers
800.477.3239 • www.lewisandroth.org